JONATHAN SWIFT

(*T. H. Mason.*)

SWIFT'S BIRTHPLACE IN HOEY'S COURT.

[Frontispiece

JONATHAN SWIFT
DEAN AND PASTOR

By

ROBERT WYSE JACKSON

 BOOKS FOR LIBRARIES PRESS
FREEPORT, NEW YORK

First Published 1939

Reprinted 1970 by arrangement with the
Right Reverend Robert Wyse Jackson

INTERNATIONAL STANDARD BOOK NUMBER:
0-8369-5581-1

LIBRARY OF CONGRESS CATALOG CARD NUMBER:
78-137380

PRINTED IN THE UNITED STATES OF AMERICA

INTRODUCTION

THIS short book is not intended to be a complete biography of Jonathan Swift. Plenty of these have been published of recent years, and some of them are very good indeed. The real purpose of these chapters is to give an outline of Swift's religious life, and to sketch something of the work which he did during his thirty-two years as Dean of St. Patrick's Cathedral, Dublin. It is particularly necessary to do this in Swift's case, because he himself was so singularly unwilling to advertise the fact that he had a religion of any sort.

At the first casual glance Swift would seem to have little interest in Christianity. It does not leap to the mind at once that Swift was a Church dignitary. Far more publicity attaches to his writings than to his Deanship. The average reader thinks of Swift as the author of *Gulliver's Travels* and as the writer of bitterly cutting and often scurrilous satires. He does not often realize that Swift was a great Dean. Yet it was the tragic contrast between the shortcomings of the world around him and the ideal of a humanity living by the Sermon on the Mount which drove him to his black misanthropy and called forth his most biting wit. The motive he described in his own verses :—

> " If he makes mankind bad as Elves,
> I answer, they may thank themselves ;
> If Vice can ever be abash'd,
> It must be Ridicul'd, or Lash'd ".

This is a side to Swift's nature which has been forgotten. Its memory was very successfully obliterated by Thackeray, but, for all that, it was very real.

The high lights in Swift's career are not ecclesiastical ones. He attained celebrity from his writings and because of his powerful political influence in Ireland. The glamour and humour of the *Drapier Letters*, and the successful resistance of Wood's Halfpence, conceal by their interest the fact that they occupied in period of time a very small fraction of his life. Nor did the comparatively small total of his literary output account for very much of his long career. Yet these two items eclipse in Swift's biographies his lengthy and quiet periods of steady Church work in the Cathedral and around the streets of Dublin. There is the secret history of a forgotten man to be written here. Happily the memory has not been quite lost. Indeed, there is a good deal of valuable and interesting material still available about Swift's religion and his churchmanship—which to him were really the most important things in life. Unfortunately, the bulk of this material is not easily accessible; it lies embedded in old biographies and histories, in cumbrous manuscript volumes still locked in St. Patrick's tower, or built into the very stones of his old Gothic church.

So here these facts have been assembled to present that other Jonathan Swift in clear daylight.

That is the reason why some of the more spectacular events in Swift's life have scarcely been mentioned here except with reference to his work as Dean. The reader will look in vain in these pages for any detailed treatment of *Gulliver's Travels* or of Swift's poetry. The *Drapier Letters* are relevant only in so far as they give a reason for the worshipping attitude of his humble parishioners, and because they throw light on his passion for justice. The long and ghastly story of Swift's last years of drivelling imbecility, toiling laboriously up and down the Deanery stairs in endless search of exercise, gazing at the mirror and murmuring pathetically, " Poor old man," is passed over in silence. They add nothing to our history. The rustling skirts of Vanessa are heard not at all; suffice it to say here that the writer is convinced that the lurid stories of Swift's guilty passion are untrue. They do not fit in with the character of the man, and for Swift they were psychologically impossible. In this matter the search for sensationalism has proved the downfall of such writers as Stephen Gwynn and Shane Leslie. Both these biographers quite misunderstood Swift's character—as do Rossi and Hone in an even worse manner.

When these few preliminary things have been said, we pass on to the fascinating picture of Swift's quiet life-work. A thrilling enough story it makes—this tale of a restless young country parson in Ulster; a garden-loving rector on the plains of Meath; a stately Dean marching to the Choir of his Cathedral behind the silver verge.

Round him circles a cavalcade of quaint and lovable figures gravitating to him by the magnetism of his personality—Roger the Clerk; gentle, raven-haired Stella; poor mad Joe Beaumont, the white-bearded linen-draper of Trim; dear, comfortable, brainless Mrs. Dingley; crabbed, gouty Prebendaries; singing-men and surpliced Vicars-choral; gentle Doctor Delaney and his wife; sly, gossiping little Mrs. Pilkington; cheering, cap-waving weavers of the Liberties; learned Doctors of the College; poor Hussey, who fell off the Cathedral ladder; Arbuthnot and Pope beyond the Irish Sea; Mr. Warburton the curate with his diligent sermons; crippled Flora the violet-seller; bishops, statesmen, beggars, scholars, workmen—friends one and all of the Dean, friends of Jonathan Swift.

BALLYMACKEY RECTORY,
NENAGH.

CONTENTS

LIST OF ILLUSTRATIONS

CHAPTER I

EARLY YEARS, MOOR PARK, KILROOT, AND DUBLIN

Hoey's Court—Birth—The Bible at Three—School and
College—Allowed a Degree—Flight to Leicester—Moor
Park and Stella—The Mystery of Swift's Marriage—
Exile in Kilroot—Moor Park Once More—Out of Work
—With Berkeley in Ireland—Meditation on a Broomstick
—A Missed Deanship—Laracor.

In Number Seven, Hoey's Court, in a high Jacobean
house in a little Dublin street not a stone's-throw
distant from St. Patrick's Cathedral, Jonathan Swift
the younger was born on November 30, 1667. He
was an Englishman, of English parents and fine old
English ancestry, but, by curious fortune, both his
birth and his greatest triumphs were staged within
the area of half a mile of Irish city. Hoey's Court was
to become legendary; innumerable corners of Ireland
still hold living traditions of the great Dean Swift;
and not a street around Dublin's oldest cathedral
exists which does not recall the stern-faced walking
pastor with his generously organized charity, the
Drapier who fought with pen and lashing tongue for
his adopted people, the uncrowned King of the Mob.

He was born into an environment of tragedy. Less
than eight months previously his father Jonathan,
steward of the King's Inns, Dublin, had died, leaving
a desperately poor widow, Abigail, and two children,
a son Thomas [1] and a little daughter Jane. Jonathan
junior was the third of the Swift family. There was

[1] Ball, *Correspondence*, Vol. IV, p. 475.

little money in that household. Jonathan Senior had enjoyed his stewardship for only fifteen months. But somehow Abigail Swift managed to exist, and a faithful old nurse from Cumberland helped her to rear her newest baby.

At only a few months old Swift made the first of many journeys across the Irish Sea. His nurse had to return to her native Whitehaven, and since she could not bear to part from her youngest charge, she kidnapped him and undertook his care for some three years. Little Jonathan must have been a precocious infant; on his own report, if we care to believe it, he was able to read any chapter of the Bible before he was three years of age.

At six years old his education was undertaken by his lawyer-speculator uncle, Godwin Swift, and he went as a boarder to that fine old Tudor foundation, Kilkenny College A fellow-pupil was William Congreve the dramatist; a few years later the gentle George Berkeley began his education at the same school.

In due course Swift passed on to Trinity College, Dublin. He was a mere schoolboy of fifteen, and his career there was not of the happiest. Even in those days he felt resentful of irksome dependence and the grind of poverty. Uncle Godwin was not more generous than he could help. " He gave me the education of a dog ", complained Swift in later years. His university days were not notably successful, and he scraped his pass degree in arts by the more than generous leniency of his examiners. His examination report could hardly have been worse—" bene ", certainly, for Greek and Latin, but " male " for philosophy and " negligenter " for theology.

Meanwhile Godwin Swift died, having previously speculated away all his wealth. And in 1688 William of Orange drove out James, and Swift, with a horde of English refugees, fled across the Channel to safety. His prospects were of the slightest. There are few jobs to be had anywhere by a penniless, badly-qualified youth of twenty-one, and for a while he was idle, living with his mother in Leicester on her tiny annuity.

Twenty pounds a year does not go far to feed four people, nor did it even in the seventeenth century. The Swift household must have been tightly pinched before Jonathan found employment. He was luckier than he realized. His mother was related to Dorothy Osborne, wife of Sir William Temple, and in 1689 Swift received the offer of a post at Moor Park. It was not much of a position for a proud and ambitious young man—twenty pounds a year and all found as a kind of secretary and literary handy-man; a position with most of the discomforts and none of the more vulgar alleviations of that of a footman. But it held the possibilities of betterment. It meant the rubbing off of the corners from " a raw and inexperienced youth ". His work brought him into contact with important people. Swift was determined to use Moor Park as a stepping-stone, for bigger things might follow if he could play his cards cleverly. He even met King William, and he felt that that introduction might lead somewhere. (Actually it led to a lesson in the art of cutting asparagus and the offer of a commission in a cavalry regiment.)

One thing which Moor Park did give him was his wonderful friendship with Stella (Esther Johnson). She was a protégée of Temple's, and it fell to his task to teach her her lessons. " I knew her from six years old," he wrote many years afterwards, " and had some share in her education by directing what books she should read, and perpetually instructing her in the principles of honour and virtue, from which she never swerved in any one action or movement of her life." [1]

Stella was the loveliest influence in Swift's life, and it was the beginning of the end for him when she died in 1728. They were married secretly in 1716 by the Bishop of Clogher in the garden of his residence. No record of the ceremony is preserved, but marriage regulations were less strict in the eighteenth century than they are now, and there is no real reason for doubting that the ceremony took place. By Dublin traditions a very similar kind of wedding is said to have been performed by Swift himself under a tree in the Phoenix Park, Dublin. At any rate, Swift's contemporaries believed that he and Stella were man and wife; it was the opinion of their close friend, Delaney, and the fact is vouched for by Bishop Evans.[2]

Yet they appear never to have lived together. We are told by authorities who had the opportunity of knowing, that they never met except in the presence of a third party. Usually this third was the ubiquitous Rebecca Dingley, the best-known and most efficient chaperon of all history. Why these two, Swift and Stella, lived this fantastic existence, can hardly be explained by any normal reasons. But Swift himself was abnormal. His mind was haunted by the tyranny of fear—dread of poverty and obscurity, nagging terror of madness. His youth had been made miserable by the bitter lack of money, so that throughout life he

---

[1] *The Character of Mrs. Johnson.*
[2] Letter by Bp. Evans, July 27, 1723. See Lecture by Abp. Bernard, February 16, 1906 (*Irish Times*).

developed an unbalanced meanness. If he forced himself to be charitable—and he did give no less than one
third of his income to the poor—he also scraped and
pinched in order to safeguard his future. The *Journal
to Stella* is full of grumbles about petty expenses :—

"By the Lord Harry, I shall be undone here with
Christmas boxes ", he complained. . . .

"It has cost me three guineas to-day for a periwig.
I am undone ! " . . .

"We dined, and it cost me above a crown. I don't
like it ! " [1]

He had been poor all his life, and his ambition
dreaded the responsibility of a wife and children, for
he had seen too many promising young men marry in
poverty and sink irrevocably, country curates on a
few pounds a year, with a horde of ragged, half-starved
children and a drudge of a wife. And these demons
of fear magnified that picture and distorted it out of
all reality, until the idea of the responsibility of marriage became a spectre to be banished at all costs.
It was not until late in life and long after he had
become a comparatively wealthy man that he actually
accepted the wedding ceremony. Even then it was a
marriage only in name. Swift lacked normal passions,
and his love for Stella was that of a son for a mother
rather than that of a man for a wife. He loved her
with a deep affection, and he grew to depend on her
woman's sympathy. Stella was always there to ease
his hours of pain, to laugh away his depressions, to
check his morbid fears. Stella took the place of a
mother for a man who needed mothering more than
anything else in the world, so that his urgent need

[1] *Journal to Stella*, December 26, 1710; January 15, 1711;
March 19, 1712.

for her revolted in hatred against that Parson Tisdall who had once wished to marry her.

In that way, Swift was sub-normal. Even the playful " Little Language " of the *Journal* was not really that of a lover. There was something old-maidish about Swift. His finicking neatness and love of petty detail; his fantastic passion for routine; his scrupulous cleanliness and fastidiousness; that prudery which degenerated to an overflow of filth, the off-scourings of a mind whose ultra niceness sickened at the normal animal functions—all these things were symptomatic of maladjustment. Perhaps here is the answer to the riddle of Swift and Stella.

A third fear placed a final barrier in the way of normal marriage. The picture of Bedlam was before his eyes always, and among that grimacing throng he saw the vacant, staring-eyed caricature of himself. Swift was not mad in the ordinary sense of the word, nor did he ever become a lunatic, but the nightmare delusion of the madhouse gates made an iron barrier between himself and Esther Johnson. Had not Uncle Godwin Swift died in a vacant, drooling stupor? That thought seared itself into his brain. How, then, could he dare to perpetuate the species of noisome Yahoo or ghastly Struldbrug?

. . . . .

By 1694 Swift was tired of his secretaryship at Moor Park and anxious for a change of sphere. According to his own account, he was unwilling to take Holy Orders merely for support, but when alternative employment in the office of the Master of the Rolls in Dublin was offered to him his conscience was cleared. He was now free to become a clergyman without feeling that he had done so only for want of more lucrative employment. The motive seems unduly subtle, but yet it is not uncharacteristic of the introspective mind of Swift. So on October 28, 1694, we find Swift ordained deacon and provided with the tiny prebend of Kilroot in the Diocese of Connor.

It was a miserably lonely and poor situation for an impatiently brilliant young man of genius. He was out of place in that windswept fishing village of dour Presbyterians, and the Established Church—*his* Church —had practically no adherents. Eighteen months of fruitless striving to win converts was enough to bring him back to Moor Park. A few shadowy legends only survive from those two foggy winters beside Belfast Lough. There is the curious tale of the wild-eyed young minister, his robes blowing in the wind, skimming stones on the water one Sunday morning to attract some sort of a congregation to church, and the kindred story of the young parson who carried boulders into Ballynure Church until a congregation followed, when the door was locked, and Jonathan Swift gave his unwilling hearers " a short and scalping " sermon. He gave up in despair, resigning his benefice and his sermons to the Reverend John Winder. " They are the most idle trifling stuff ever written ", he said contemptuously of these compositions. Very probably they were. The sort of half-civilized fisherman congregation he had in Kilroot certainly neither needed nor desired anything deep or literary.

From 1696 Swift continued at Moor Park until Temple's death in 1699. He was again thrown on his own resources, with a rather scrappy stock-in-trade, consisting of a small legacy, the work of editing Temple's manuscripts, a vague promise from William of the first vacant prebend at Westminster or Canter-

B

bury, and a mild literary reputation as the author of some Pindaric Odes. (Of these Dryden commented, " Cousin Swift, you will never be a poet ! ") The most hopeful asset was the King's promise. But after some months' delay Swift discovered that the notorious untrustworthiness of princes had not been exaggerated, for, taking the line of least resistance, King William did nothing, and he showed no signs of ever intending to help.

At this juncture there came to Swift an invitation from the Earl of Berkeley to accompany him to Ireland as chaplain and private secretary. The combined post was a good one, but it lasted only until the arrival at Dublin, when the secretaryship was taken away from Swift in favour of another candidate. Swift's only work now was to read prayers in the household of the Lord Justice and to minister to Lady Berkeley's somewhat affected piety.

It was to this same lady that five years later he solemnly read a remarkable sermonette ! Lady Berkeley had developed a liking for Mr. Boyle's short Meditations—in fact thoroughly sugary and artificial productions. Whenever he was in London, Swift found himself called to her boudoir to read her some of these publications. It was a thoroughly distasteful task for him, and their all-too-obvious synthetic piety bored and exasperated him, for religious hypocrisy then, as always, was to him the worst of crimes. One day the Reverend Doctor Swift read to her devout ladyship a Meditation which immensely struck her fancy. It had the solemn (and, dare one say, singsong?) cadences of Mr. Boyle's musings, but it seemed to her to be far above the average for ingenuity, for depth of thought, and for intensity of feeling. " How wonderful dear Mr. Boyle is ! " she said to herself. " Imagine writing such a beautiful meditation on a broomstick ! "

We can well imagine the solemn-faced young chaplain gravely intoning the periods, chuckling inwardly :—

> " When I beheld this I sighed and said within myself, surely mortal Man is a Broomstick ; Nature sent him into the world strong and lusty in a thriving condition, wearing his own Hair on his Head, the proper Branches of this reasoning Vegetable, till the Axe of Intemperance has lopp'd off his green Boughs, and left him a wither'd Trunk : He then flies to Art and puts on a Periwig, valuing himself upon an unnatural Bundle of Hairs, all covered with Powder that never grew on his Head, but now should this our Broomstick pretend to enter the Scene, proud of those Birchen spoils it never bore, and all covered with dust, though the sweeping of the finest Lady's Chamber, we should be apt to ridicule and despise its vanity. Partial judges that we are of our own Excellencies, and other Men's Defaults ! "

Lady Berkeley did not suspect the parody until a friend found the manuscript in Swift's writing inserted into the volume. To her credit, she enjoyed the joke—but Swift never again had to suffer the discomfort of reading aloud the insufferable Boyle !

During this earlier chaplaincy in Dublin the loss of the secretaryship was succeeded by a second disappointment. The Deanery of Derry came vacant, and Swift had been promised the first vacant benefice. Derry was a prize worth having, and Swift must have hoped for success. But the Reverend John Bolton of Laracor was also in search of the dignity, and it had been hinted to him that £1000 would ease his election.

The upshot of the affair was obvious—Swift would not get the deanery of Derry, since he certainly did not possess £1000. He dismissed the simoniacal pair who had bested him with a fervent and comprehensive malediction, and he could not be appeased even by the ingenious fictions of his noble patron, who quoted an imaginary letter from the Bishop of Derry saying that Swift was too young and too likely to be making interminable excursions out of his Cathedral Close to the more exciting atmosphere of London. Accordingly, since Berkeley saw that, for comfort's sake, something must be done for his turbulent young chaplain, Bolton's vacant livings were handed over to him as a consolation prize. Thus Swift came to Laracor.

(*T. H. Mason*)

LARACOR OLD CHURCH.

[Facing p. 11

CHAPTER II

SWIFT IN LARACOR

Laracor, Agher, and Rathbeggan—The Old Parish Church—
Roger the Clerk—The Curate and Congregation—
Parochial Differences—Dissent at Summerhill—Mr. Nuttall
—The Oldest Inhabitant—Poor Joe—The Vicarage
House—Swift's Garden and Trout Stream—Parochial
Improvements—Decline and Fall of Laracor.

ON March 22, 1699, Swift was instituted to the
Rectory of Agher and the Vicarages of Laracor
and Rathbeggan, all in the Diocese of Meath, which
with the Prebend of Dunlavin gave him an income of
about £244 per annum—a fair income in those days,
when a curate could be " passing rich on forty pounds
a year ". (As a matter of fact this same sum was
the stipend paid by Swift to his own curate.)

Laracor was the principal parish in the union. No
definite information seems to be available as to whether
the church of Agher was in use in Swift's time. A
Visitation of the Diocese made in 1723 notes that this
parish had been episcopally united to Laracor, and
that while one part of it was convenient to Laracor
Church, another detached portion was more than five
miles distant. No church is mentioned. But in 1747,
two years after Swift's death, a chalice was presented
to Agher by Hercules Langford, which suggests that
at any rate the parish church must have been in use
at that period. By 1818 the building had become
ruinous, and it was being extensively reconstructed.

These two Crown livings were united with the small

parish of Rathbeggan, whose patron was the Earl of Drogheda. This church—a ruinous little building— was served by a Mr. Jordan, the neighbouring vicar of Dunshaughlin. At the beginning of the nineteenth century the glebe and church were rebuilt, and the parish carried on an independent existence until 1882, when it was served once more by the Rector of Dunshaughlin. Services are no longer held in the church.

Laracor Old Church has long since vanished; the present church was built about 1860. But a picture of the old church exists which was published in the *Illustrated London News* some eighty or ninety years ago, and there are traditional descriptions of its interior. It was a low, rugged little slated building, constructed in no particular style of ecclesiastical architecture—on the whole it bears the marks of local seventeenth-century design. Above the west wall stood a vast chimney to accommodate a turf fire. A little gabled porch stood also at the west end. The north side was dominated by a relatively immense vestry. Square doors and windows completed this quite un-churchlike little preaching-house.

The interior was furnished after the style customary in the period. The Visitation of 1723 describes " a handsome well built Church in very decent repair, the Church and Chancel ceiled and flagged and furnished with all conveniences except a Surplice and Carpet ". At the east end was the crude, uncovered, semicircular communion table, now preserved in St. Patrick's Cathedral, Dublin, and still used for its original purpose. In the body of the church were a few horse-box pews for the leading families, and two or three free seats at the back for the poorer members of the congregation. The more easterly pews had seats facing in two directions—eastwards to the Communion-table, westwards to the big three-decker pulpit half-way along the north wall of the church. From his reading-desk under the pulpit Swift would pass into the big square vestry to the north of the building, and so up steps from thence to deliver the sermon. At a still lower level sat Roger the Clerk, jealous of his privilege of answering the responses and leading the singing—that is, if Swift's half score of congregation, "all gentle and most simple", were capable of sustaining a tune ! Swift himself would have been of no assistance—he was thoroughly unmusical. Perhaps his curate made good the deficiency !

The parish clerk, Roger Cox, figures largely in those vague traditional jokes which have attached to Swift, as they have to all celebrated wits. In his red waistcoat and grey tail-coat, Roger was something of a figure. Lord Orrery tells one story, which is probably true, about him and his rector—at any rate it sounds characteristic of Swift.

When Swift came first to Laracor he decided to augment the Sunday service with weekday services on Wednesdays and Fridays—a fairly common practice now, but rare indeed in eighteenth-century country parishes. Unfortunately, on the first Wednesday none of Swift's handful of parishioners responded—except of course Roger, who ex officio was bound to attend. The bell stopped ringing and Roger took his place at the lower reading-desk. Swift waited for a few minutes. No one came. Then he solemnly started the service. "Dearly Beloved Roger, the scripture moveth you and me in sundry places", he began, and he proceeded in that manner through the service !

Apparently Swift and Roger found one another

satisfactory fellow-workers—they agreed in religion and politics, their dispositions were not dissimilar, and each was a wit in his own way. To use Roger's own phrase, " the pulpit and the reading-desk are always on the best terms, although we have word about with each other ".

Little else is known of Roger, except that he was a convivial soul, a welcome guest at weddings and wakes, and something of a poet, modelling his work on that of Samuel Butler—and, no doubt, on Swift. Three or four of his poems have been preserved. One is an amorous ditty entitled " The Deserted Fair ". Two of them, " The Landlord " and " Interest, like Rust ", are concerned with financial embarrassment. The latter set of verses contains an amusing couplet which reminds us of Sundays in Laracor Church :—

> " So sure as Swift sticks to his text,
> So sure I'll pay you Monday next ".

Perhaps the most interesting of Roger's poems is that which was inscribed in the marriage register of Laracor, and which describes the performance of a country wedding by Swift. The latter portion of the verses are quoted here :—

> " They both were tied by Dr. Swift,
> And Kate had put on her best shift;
> With cap and handkerchief as white
> As snow on a December night,
> And Ned was drest just as he should be,
> In home-spun cloth as neat as could be.
> The roses bloom'd on Kitty's cheek—
> Dear, I could think of her a week;
> So young, so innocent and fair,
> I never saw so blest a pair.
> This marriage, sure, was made in Heaven,
> And free from matrimonial leaven;
> To see some brides, whom I have seen,
> Eat up with vanity and spleen,

As Hymen, with a sickly torch,
Conducts them into the porch;
The groom, as he approached the altar,
Appeared to drag her with a halter,
And scarcely seated in her carriage
Not half an hour after marriage,
In spite of all her sacred vows,
Of soft submission to her spouse
She claimed the breeches as her due,
And wore them from that moment, too.
But, Ned, thy case was different quite,
Hymen for thee prepar'd a light,
A saffron robe, a smokeless torch,
Nor did he quit you in the porch,
You never thought of line or halter,
With modest steps, you sought the altar,
You led on Kate, and nothing loath,
The Doctor smil'd upon you both :
I love to see the Doctor smile,
For it's the sunshine of our Isle ". . . .

It is very pleasant to be given a glimpse of Swift's smile—very few people other than Roger have described it for us.

Another of Swift's flock was the worthy Mr. Thomas Warburton, the curate. After a preliminary meeting when Swift had behaved brusquely and overbearingly to test poor Warburton's humility they became firm friends, and Swift nicknamed him " Sub ". On week-days Warburton taught school in Trim, though not with any great profit, for it was "but a thin school ".[1] Swift unsuccessfully tried to obtain for Warburton a prebend in St. Patrick's. He described him as a man who " behaved altogether unblamably and as a gentleman of very good learning and sense ". Later Mr. Warburton married a rich wife and became a prosperous rector in the North of Ireland. He was a good preacher, and Swift found it hard to replace him.[2] In

[1] Letter, July 8, 1713.
[2] Letter, January 27, 1716–17.

the eighteenth century a capable curate was more precious than rubies—they were all too rare. Swift appreciated the merits of a good curate, and he sympathized with his difficulties in those days of understaffed country benefices. It may be worth quoting here a few lines which he wrote on the subject—they are not dissimilar in vein from Roger's own verses. They are entitled " On a Curate's Complaint of Hard Duty ".

> " I march'd three miles through scorching sand,
> With zeal in heart and notes in hand ;
> I rode four more to Great St. Mary,
> Using four legs, when two were weary :
> To three fair virgins I did tie men,
> In the close bonds of pleasing Hymen ;
> I dipp'd two babes in holy water,
> And purified their mother after.
> Within an hour and eke a half,
> I preach'd three congregations deaf."

> " My emblem, the laborious sun,
> Saw all these mighty labours done
> Before one race of his was run.
> All this perform'd by Robert Hewit :
> What mortal else could e'er go through it."

The community of Laracor was a tiny one, small even for those days of scattered churchpeople. " There are but few Protestant families in the Parish ", notes the 1723 Visitation. Happily it adds the saving clause, " but some are very wealthy " !

The three leading families and their characteristics were summed up amusingly in a letter to Stearne : " Mr. Percival is Ditching, Mrs. Percival in her Kitchen, Mr. Wesley Switching, Mrs. Wesley Stitching, Sir Arthur Langford Riching ".[1]

Garret Wesley of Dangan was a member of Parlia-

---

[1] Letter, April 17, 1710.

ment for the borough of Trim and later for the county.
He died in 1728, and by will he bequeathed his estate
to his cousin, Richard Colley, the ancestor of the Duke
of Wellington. Laracor graveyard was the family
burying-place, and there was in the old church of
Laracor a handsome tablet giving an appreciation of
his services to Church and State. (This is now in the
modern Laracor Church.) He was the donor of the
present Communion silver.

Wesley and Swift were firm friends. The same cannot be said of all the families. Among his handful of
parishioners there were some who were a source of
annoyance. With two at least Swift came into conflict, and these of the leading families. One was
Robert Percival, who in 1718 had succeeded his father,
Swift's old friend and neighbour, as M.P. for Trim.
This gentleman seized the thinnest of excuses to deprive Swift of half his tithes, a matter of some fifty
shillings a year. Swift protested—vigorously, we may
be sure—and received an answer which elicited a counter
reply in the Dean's most scurrilous vein.[1]

> " I told my friend [he wrote] that from the
> badness of your educations, and from the cast of
> your nature . . . I expected nothing from you
> that became a gentleman, that I had expostulated
> this scurvy matter very gently with you; that I
> conceived this letter was an answer; that from
> the prerogative of a good estate however gotten,
> and the practice of lording over a few Irish
> wretches, and from the natural want of better
> thinking, I was sure your answer would be ex-
> tremely rude and stupid; full of very bad language
> in all senses."

[1] Letter, January 3, 1729–30.

He went on to deplore the greedy character of all Irish squires, regretfully comparing his own care for the finances of Laracor parish, " who gave among you fifty years purchase for land, for which I am not to see one farthing. This was intended as an encouragement to a clergyman to reside among you, whenever any of your posterity shall be able to distinguish a man from a beast."

This truly remarkable example of pastoral epistle closes with the threat that it is to appear in print (one of Swift's favourite weapons), and with a devastating reminder to Percival to learn to know his place. " I never imagined you so utterly devoid of knowing some little distinction between persons ", concludes Swift. This production must be unique as an example of a letter from a country parson to his squire—but in 1730 this particular parson was also the Drapier, and the most powerful and the most feared figure in the kingdom !

An earlier conflict with one of the great landowners of Laracor was that with Sir Arthur Langford of Summerhill. As early as 1683 there is mention of a Presbyterian chapel at the seat of this family, and Sir Arthur was an ardent supporter of the rival faction. Swift objected strongly, writing to Langford on October 30, 1704, that " the most moderate churchman may be apt to resent, when they see a sect, without toleration or law, insulting the established religion " ! It was in this same year, 1704, that *The Tale of a Tub* appeared, with its virulent satellite, the " Essay on the Mechanical Operation of the Spirit ", attached to it. Not improbably the Summerhill conventicle gave some additional sting to this latter pamphlet against the Nonconformist sects !

Dissent within his own parish must have been more than galling to Swift—his Kilroot experiences, too, had embittered him against all Presbyterians. Nor did he succeed in ridding himself of the rival congregation, for in later years we hear of Langford having left a rent charge of £30 per annum towards the maintenance of a Presbyterian minister at his private chapel. The Visitation of 1723 notes, too, " There is in the Parish of Larachor, viz. at Summerhill, a Meeting house served by a Presbyterian teacher who lives there. There is support for it left by Sir Arthur Longford." This chapel was in existence until the very end of the nineteenth century.

No doubt the Presbyterian feeling in Swift's Laracor union of benefices coloured that paragraph in his last will, where he left the tithes of the parish of Effernock, near Trim, to the vicars of Laracor for so long as the Episcopal religion continued to be established. He had bought these tithes at his own expense for the sum of £260, and by a special clause he made it a condition that if any other form of Christianity should become the established faith in Ireland, the money should cease to go to the vicar, and should be made over to the poor of Laracor in instalments payable weekly, " excepting professed Jews, infidels, and atheists ".

Besides the three wealthy families of Wesley, Langford, and Percival, there were a few other folk under Swift's care. For instance, there was a certain Mr. Nuttall, whom he was able to help in London in 1712. " I went over this morning with a parishioner of mine, one Nuttall, who came over here for a legacy of one hundred pounds," wrote Swift, " and a roguish lawyer had refused to pay him, and would not believe he was the man. I writ to the lawyer a sharp letter that I had taken Nuttall into my protection, and was resolved to stand by him; and the next news was, that the lawyer desired I would meet him, and attest he was the man, which I did, and his money was paid upon the spot." [1]

Then there was the oldest inhabitant, " Goodman Bomford "—otherwise Lawrence Bomford of Clonmahon in Laracor, who died in 1720 at the remarkable age of 103. There was Patrick Dollan of Clondoogan.[2] Sometimes, too, Stella and her faithful shadow, Mrs. Dingley, came to hear Swift preach in Laracor Old Church. On these visits they stayed in a cottage near Trim which still stands.

We have almost reached the end of the list of Swift's tiny congregation. To complete the parish roll comes only one more name—that of the inimitable Joe Beaumont.

" Poor Joe " was an eccentric shopkeeper in Trim with a tendency towards higher mathematics and a particular fondness for longitudes. In due course he went slightly mad.[3] Swift got an enormous amount of fun out of Joe, but he was genuinely fond of him, and he went out of his way to assist him. " I am heartily concerned for poor Joe ", he wrote, when the unfortunate linendraper had gone off his head. " I am endeavouring to persuade Joe that he is mad. I have given him twenty shillings to buy a periwig."

Sometimes Joe was a real responsibility, as when he appeared suddenly " mad in London, riding through the streets on his Irish horse with all the Rabble after him, and throwing his money among them ". On that

[1] *Journal to Stella*, January 5, 1712.
[2] Letter, July 8, 1713.
[3] Letter, January 31, 1716–17.

occasion Swift had to secure him and lock him up safely in Bedlam. Joe's finances, too, must have cost Swift a good deal of money—Swift bought all kinds of unnecessary articles from him in order to keep him going. Twenty pounds' worth of soap, a four-pound horse and twenty-four yards of linen at £6 8s. were among the transactions. When he died he left the Dean with the responsibility of winding up his disordered estate—no easy task, from anything that we can read of Joe.

Although the material on Swift's parochial work must needs be scanty, one little item from his own private accounts gives us a hint as to what his people meant to him. Although he was yet poor he was able to anticipate a later scheme in a small way, giving away £80 in small loans to poor tradespeople about Trim to help them in business—a thankless and no doubt ill-repaid bounty !

Less than a day's journey from Laracor was Quilca, near Virginia Water in the County of Cavan. This was the home of Swift's happy-go-lucky schoolmaster friend, Dr. Thomas Sheridan, and his scolding wife, and here Swift often spent his summer holidays. The house still stands—less dilapidated now than it was in Swift's day, when it seems to have been in the very last stages of disrepair. The Dean has left a humorous description of its shortcomings, and among his lesser grumbles were :—

"The kitchen perpetually crowded with savages."
" Not a bit of mutton to be had in the country."
" Want of beds and a mutiny thereupon among the servants until supplied from Kells."

The townland of Mullagh where Quilca stands is still crowded with Swift traditions. For these I am

indebted to Philip O'Connell, Esq., of Clonmel. At
Quilca there is " Stella's Bower " and " Swift's Well ",
and in the lake is a small island called " Swift's Island ".
It is said that on one occasion, during Sheridan's
absence, Swift employed a band of local labourers in
heaping up stones in the lake to build an artificial
island, on which he planted shrubs. This was in order
to give his host a surprise on his return ! (Swift
was given to drastic and usually unauthorized feats
of landscape gardening on the estates of his acquaintances.)

Close by is a circle of trees planted by Sheridan to
make an open-air theatre which was used by Swift
and his friends for very amateur dramatics. Also on
the estate is a rath or mound where Swift is said to
have written part of *Gulliver's Travels* during the
summers of 1724 and 1725.

The germ of the *Travels* had been thought of years
before, but they did not begin to be written until
Swift received the immediate urge that first summer
holiday at Quilca. The direct inspiration came from
a local giant known as " Big Doughty ". He was a
farmer of huge stature—so great, indeed, that on one
occasion he rescued a man who was wanted by the
sheriff's officer, by the expedient of concealing him
under his great-coat until the pursuer had passed by.
Doughty appears to have been a kind of County Cavan
Robin Hood—thus, he was responsible for lifting a
widow's cow out of the village pound and setting it
free. For the special entertainment of the Dean he
gave an exhibition of his powers, taking a pony in his
arms and carrying it about the fields and over the
fences of the estate. Swift was immensely impressed,
and it was undoubtedly the great stature of Big

Doughty which gave him the impetus to begin writing his famous story.

Laracor continued to be held by Swift until his death; he was vicar there for no less than forty-six years. He loved the quiet homeliness of the place, and even when Dean, he spent much time there. Bishop Pococke, writing in 1752, notes that he used to spend a month or two in the summer " in a little house " near the church. He indulged his passion for exercise by riding and gardening, and it was convenient for Dublin, being within the day's journey.

When Swift was appointed to the living, the parsonage had been practically derelict. The vicar's house was tiny, a mere cottage. Swift called the glebe itself " half an acre of Irish bog ", and in 1714 he gave a jesting description of the conditions of his estate. " The wall of my apartment is fallen down," he said, " and I want mud to rebuild it, and straw to thatch it. Besides, a spiteful neighbour has seized on six feet of ground, carried off my trees, and spoiled my grove." However, Swift improved the poor original out of all recognition. He made the house comfortable, enclosed a garden, and built a high brick wall with a southern aspect for the cultivation of fruit trees. (The erection of garden walls was one of Swift's minor passions; he did the same thing for the Deanery.)

For such a colourless document, the Visitation seems quite enthusiastic about Swift's improvements.

> " The original glebe belonging to the Parish contains about an acre and is exceedingly well enclosed. There is a good garden and a neat cabin made by the present incumbent, Value £60, situated near the Church."

C

A little stream flowed past the parsonage. Swift had had some experience of Dutch landscape gardening—Moor Park gardens were notable examples. He modelled Laracor garden into a small imitation; the stream was dammed, and a walled fish-pond was made and stocked with fish. Beside the stream, under the willows, he made a little walk, described enthusiastically by Delaney in his *Observations*. The garden, said his biographer, was very pretty, and he had smoothed the banks of its boundary stream, where he had what he called his Margine Ripae, a charming path following the windings of the water, " from whence I apprehend he copied that part of his wish in that imitation of Horace, Lib. 2, Sat. 6.

> " ' A handsome house to lodge a friend,
> A river at my garden's end;
> A terrass-walk, and half a rood
> Of land, set out to plant a wood.' " [1]

Laracor was perhaps the one place where Swift could be happy; he could relax there after the stress and strain of London politics and cathedral battles, and he could forget everything except his cherry trees and his speckled trout. When things were at their hardest, Laracor soothed and refreshed him. When he was stifled in the hot streets and close brick walls of London, the vision of the cool green of his meadow and the ripples of his little river came back to him, tantalized him. During his London commission to secure the grant of the First Fruits from the Government he ached to see the yellow-gosling down of his willows.

> " O that we were at Laracor this fine day!
> The willows begin to peep, and the quicks to bud.

[1] Delaney, p. 193.

ESTHER JOHNSON.

From the painting by Charles Jervais in the National Portrait Gallery,
Dublin.

[Facing p. 25

My dream is out; I was a dreaming last night that I ate ripe cherries. And now they begin to catch the pikes, and will shortly the trouts, and I would fain know whether the floods were ever so high as to get over the Holly bank or the river walk; if so, then all my pike are gone, but I hope not." [1]

That is the true lyrical touch, and Laracor only could bring it out in Swift—his own Laracor, like Marvell's garden,

> " Annihilating all that's made
>   To a green thought in a green shade ".

" Don't you begin to see the flowers and blossoms of the field? How busy should I be now at Laracor ! " [2]

And when he lay sick in his city lodging, attended only by his drunken servant Patrick, his hot and throbbing brain carried him away over the Irish sea to that little garden in Meath. " Oh my poor willows and quicksets ! " he cried.

At last he returned—came back to a big, ugly, rambling mansion in the slums of Dublin. And to Laracor he fled for solace. " I prefer a field bed and an earthen floor before the great house they say is mine." And looking out of the little window of his thatched cottage he was happy to see his quiet garden and the prim, grey, country church beyond. " My river walk is extremely pretty, and my canal in great beauty, and I see trout in it." [3] And for a brief while he was at peace.

The quiet little parish held such a place in Swift's

---

[1] *Journal to Stella*, March 19, 1711.
[2] *Ibid.*, March 26, 1711.
[3] Letter, July 8, 1713.

affections that he resolved to improve it and to provide it with an endowment for ever. In 1716 he purchased twenty acres of glebe land by means of a grant of £200 from the trustees of the First Fruits, expressing in the deed that the grant had been given in consideration of his instrumentality in securing the whole fund for the benefit of the Church of Ireland.[1] A month later he divulged to Archbishop King that he was planning another scheme. He intended to rent a further twenty-three acres from a local landlord, in consideration of a first personal payment of £55, and a rent in perpetuity of £14 per annum. In addition, he intended to lay out £200 from his own pocket to improve the glebe house. It was a generous gesture —the only loser was Swift himself. " Everybody approves the thing, since it is a good bargain for the Church, a better for the gentleman, and only a bad one for myself." [2]

Here Swift's enthusiasm outran his caution, and in his reply the Archbishop pointed out how the Dean's benefaction might come to nothing under future careless vicars. " Pray take some care ", he wrote. To his mind the probable sequel would be that generations to come would allow the residence to go out of repair, and that they would neglect to pay the rent for ten or twelve years, when the landlord would re-enter and seize the property.[3] Apparently Swift took the warning, for the extra land was not rented.

Perhaps it is just as well, for Archbishop King's prophecy was not far from what actually happened. The sequel is described in Bishop O'Beirne's MSS. of

[1] Letter to Archbishop King, November 13, 1716.
[2] *Ibid.*, December 22, 1716.
[3] Letter from Archbishop King, January 12, 1717.

1815 on the State of the Diocese of Meath—a document which speaks for itself :—

" The ruins of a cabin which Dean Swift built on it, and in which he sometimes resided, still remain. During his incumbency, and partly by grant from the Trustees of the First Fruits, and partly at his private expense, as appears by one of his letters, a glebe was purchased of what now measures 21 acres, with a view to having a glebe house built on it. But nothing was done during his incumbency, or that of his successor, who lived to the year 1799. The succession of incumbents was so rapid for some years after, that all injunctions for building were evaded, and it was not until the year 1813 that a substantial house was completed."

And a few years later Swift's little house was a farmer's cottage, and his lovingly cherished garden a potato-patch.

CHAPTER III

" THE TALE OF A TUB "

The Tale of a Tub—Its Authorship—A Young Man's Book—Iconoclasm—Contents of the Tale—Peter, Jack, and Martin—Swift's Intolerance—His Opinion of Roman Catholicism—of Dissent—The Test Act—of Deism—Logic *versus* Revelation—Freethinking—Matthew Tindal—The Demolition of Collins.

JUST four years after Swift's institution at Laracor there appeared a book which both sealed his reputation as a literary genius and helped very materially to ruin his chances of preferment. In 1704 *The Tale of a Tub* was published, after having been laid aside for some seven or eight years.

This fantastic, brilliantly savage work caused an immediate sensation—it was the most provocative book of the age, and it was obvious that a new and biting pen was about to steal the literary stage. The book appeared anonymously, and at first rumour attributed the authorship to all kinds of people—even Swift's " little parson cousin ", Thomas, was suggested as a possible author, and he almost gained preferment on the strength of his wit. But soon the authorship fastened itself to Swift, and although he never expressly acknowledged it, there is no doubt that the *Tale* came from his pen.

It was a grossly outspoken and irreverent work. It has been the fashion for critics to tone down its ferocity against the background of a coarse Hogarthian age, and to plead in extenuation that it won the

laughers over to Swift's side in defence of the Established Religion. Perhaps it did—but such laughers
would be uncomfortable allies for the Church of England. And those who have been accused of being
prudes were in the right.

Religious people were genuinely shocked. Swift's old
enemy, the Duchess of Somerset (" carrots " to him !),
and Archbishop Sharpe quoted it to a devout if insipid
queen as proof that the Vicar of Laracor was an atheist,
and so must not be promoted to a bishopric. We can
hardly blame Queen Anne for accepting the suggestion.

But Swift himself was sincere when he wrote in an
apology some years afterwards that he would forfeit
his life if any one opinion could be fairly deduced
from that book which was contrary to religion or
morality. His treatment of the Established Church
was not ungentle, if somewhat ribald, and he could not
see that in hitting at the abuses of religion he appeared to
strike at the most fundamental doctrines of Christianity.

One clue to the mind of the author of *The Tale of a
Tub* is that it was a young man's book. Swift had set
out with the brutality and insensitiveness of a very
young man to achieve novelty. There had been so
many boring books published, and his at least must
not be dull ! That fact he admitted with an apologetic
note :—

> " He was then a young gentleman much in the
> world, and wrote to the taste of those who were
> like himself; therefore, in order to allure them,
> he gave a liberty to his pen which might not suit
> with maturer years or graver characters, and which
> he could easily have corrected with a very few blots,
> had he been master of his papers for a year or two
> before their publication."

The bulk of the *Tale* had been completed by 1696, when he was under thirty years of age. Some of it had been seen in manuscript at Kilroot, when Swift was twenty-seven—or even, according to one story, when he was a student at Trinity College.

And that must be Swift's excuse, if excuse is possible, for the manner of the book. Its roughshod coarseness and its irreverence were things which the years mellowed in the man. But its sincerity lasted throughout his life.

Irresistibly we are reminded of the dashing young parson, who was keen enough to have weekday services in an obscure " hedge parish ", but could not resist the " dearly beloved Roger " jest. The *Tale* has that juvenile sort of sharp cleverness which passes away with maturity. In later years Swift himself could read it as something outside his own middle-aged scope. Youth had passed away, and Swift could read it as the work of another man, and exclaim, " Good God, what a genius I had when I wrote that book ! "

Old age learns reverence, and, for all his lack of reticence, the Dean of St. Patrick's would not and could not have written the *Tale* as it was first written. Can we not picture the old Dean closing the book with an affectionate smile of reminiscence murmuring, " What a brilliant young puppy I was, to be sure ", and reaching for his writing tablets to note down sententiously, " If a man would register all his opinions upon Love, Politicks, Religion, Learning, etc., beginning from his youth, and so go on to old age, what a Bundle of Inconsistencies and Contradictions would appear at last " ? [1]

It is wise to remember that a man's character changes

[1] *Thoughts on Various Subjects.*

and develops—too often superficial critics of Swift
have quoted the style of this book of 1696 as proof of
the insincerity and irreverence of the Dean of later
years.

Having said this much, it must be added to complete
the picture that the underlying motive of the book
remained with Swift until the very end of his seventy-
eight years. He hated the shams and hypocrisies
and corruptions of mankind, and he castigated them as
devastatingly in his old age under the guise of Lilli-
putians and Brobdingnagians and Laputans and
Yahoos as he had ever done in his youth in the persons
of Jack and Peter. For although Swift believed firmly
in the goodness of God, yet he never learned to see the
corresponding goodness in God's creation, mankind.
Swift was no optimist, and he saw all too clearly the
tragically low standards of the society around him.
Too often the fumes of his fiery indignation hid the
world's few poor virtues from his eyes, so that he could
focus nothing but the sin and suffering. The average
man, while perhaps agreeing with Article IX, that
" man is very far gone from original righteousness,
and is of his own nature inclined to evil ", is optimist
enough to add that, on the whole, the world is not too
bad. Swift could not do this. He must flay the covering of shams from society and show the ugly meanness
underneath. He must shock the world into repentance.
That was his self-appointed mission. Yet his pessimism
showed him that his labours would be useless ; that the
work would be too great for him, and that knowledge
again poured the poison of despair into his pen.

In its final form *The Tale of a Tub* is the most dis-
cursive book ever written. Before we reach the narrative
at all we are provided with an Analytical Table—surely

nowhere more necessary!—a Postscript; a List of
Fictitious Treatises; the Booksellers' Dedication to
Lord Somers; the Bookseller to the Reader; a Dedica-
tion to Posterity; a Preface and an Introduction.
Through the story there are sundry Digressions;
a Dissertation on Madness; the Author's compliments
to the Readers, and a Conclusion. Few could blame
Dr. Johnson for calling it " That wild book ".

The kernel of the story consists of the adventures
of Peter, Jack, and Martin, representing respectively
the Pope, Calvin, and Luther, or the Roman Catholics,
the Dissenters, and the Church of England.

The three brothers start each with a new coat provided by their father, with a will to explain just how
it should be worn. After a while each begins to em-
bellish his coat with decorations of which the father
had never dreamed, and ingenious indeed are their feats
of exegesis and logic to provide sanctions for the wearing
of shoulder-knots, embroidered figures, gold lace, and
silver fringes! Then Peter becomes inordinately
proud, takes to wearing three hats at once, and develops
the unpleasant trick of kicking his acquaintances in
the mouth by way of a salute. Eventually he goes
completely mad; he serves up crusts of brown bread
to his brothers and insists with mighty oaths that they
are best Leadenhall mutton and true natural juice
from the grape, and he deals in raree-shows, ferocious
bulls, whispering offices, and sundry other crazy
fancies.

Here the satire becomes thoroughly offensive, and,
to tell the truth, tedious in its multiplied skits on
Purgatory, the Saints, Indulgences, Holy Water,
Transubstantiation, Relics, Celibacy of the Clergy,
and a score of other Roman dogmas and customs.

In course of time Jack and Martin quarrel with Peter, and decide to strip their coats of the embellishments they had added under Peter's influence. Jack Calvin begins to tear them off so feverishly that in a short time he has reduced his coat to shreds, and, angry and remorseful, he too falls into " the oddest whimseys that ever a sick brain conceived "—eccentricities of the Fanatics and Independents not spared by Swift's scurrilous pen !

But Martin values his coat too much to risk damaging the original fabric. And so he works cautiously :—

> " Resolving therefore to rid his coat of a huge quantity of gold lace, he picked up the stitches with much caution, and diligently gleaned out all the loose threads as he went, which proved to be a work of time. Then he fell about the embroidered Indian figures of men, women, and children, against which, as you have heard in its due place, their father's testament was extremely exact and severe ; these with much dexterity and application, were, after a while, quite eradicated or utterly defaced. For the rest, where he observed the embroidery to be worked so close as not to be got away without damaging the cloth, or where it served to hide or strengthen any flaw in the body of the coat, contracted by the perpetual tampering of workmen upon it, he concluded the wisest course was to let it remain, resolving in no case whatsoever that the substance of the stuff should suffer injury; which he thought the best method for serving the true intent and meaning of his father's will."

It must be admitted that Martin gets off much more lightly than his other brothers, and that he escapes the brunt of the satire against Jack and Peter. The author himself says that the story of Martin " celebrates the Church of England as the most perfect of all others in discipline and doctrine; it advances no opinion they reject, nor condemns any they receive ". But the reader who is an enthusiastic supporter of the Establishment may be excused for finding the subsequent history of Martin less inspiring than he would like it to be. Nor perhaps would Anglicans be inclined to be over-grateful to Swift for his account of the Elizabethan settlement. " Lady Bess " trimmed for some time between Peter and Martin, at the same time casting a friendly eye at Jack. Then she saw that she could not possibly reconcile the three, and set up an apothecary's shop of her own well stocked with powders, plasters, and salves stolen from the receipt books of all three brothers. Her ministers " of this medley or hodge podge made up a dispensatory of their own, strictly forbidding any other to be used, and particularly Peter's, from which the greatest part of this new dispensatory was stolen ".

To the modern reader the ugliest side of all this is the intolerance—but without condoning we have to remember that religious toleration can scarcely be said to have existed at the beginning of the eighteenth century.

Swift tolerated neither Roman Catholicism nor the various forms of Dissent which he threw together in the contemptuous catalogue, " Deism, Atheism, Socinianism, Quakerism, Muggletonianism, Fanaticism, Brownism ".[1]

He would have given a great deal to have seen his friend Pope sincerely converted from a religion which he despised. Swift had no respect for Romanism;

[1] *Roman Catholic's Reason for Repealing the Test.*

to him it did not even constitute a great problem.
The terrible days of the 1641 rising were passing out
of the memories of the eighteenth-century Protestant
rulers of Ireland. Swift considered the Roman
Catholic majority in Ireland too weak to be a menace.
Penal Acts had ensured that the property of substantial
Roman Catholic landowners should progressively be
subdivided, until it had all been reduced to tiny hold-
ings owned by miserable peasants. It appeared to
Swift not improbable that the Established Religion
in due time would sweep the country.

> " The popish priests are all registered, and with-
> out permission which I hope will not be granted,
> they can have no successors; so that the protestant
> clergy will find it perhaps no difficult matter to
> bring great numbers over to the church; and in
> the meantime the common people, without leaders,
> without discipline or natural courage, being little
> better than hewers of wood and drawers of water,
> are out of all capacity of doing any mischief,
> if they were ever so well inclined ".[1]

Actually, however, the eighteenth-century Church
of Ireland proved itself so lacking in energy and in
missionary fire that no great movements towards the
Establishment ever materialized. So far was it from
strengthening its own position, that the close of the
century saw widespread neglect of pastoral ministrations
even among its own people. Many southern parishes
to-day preserve traditions of the first-fruits of the
nineteenth-century Evangelical Revivial—mass bap-
tisms and marriages of whole communities which had
been deserted by their clergy for years on end.
More bitter than his dislike for Romanism was

[1] *Letter Concerning the Sacramental Test*, 1708.

Swift's feeling towards the Dissenters. As we have seen, his own parochial experiences brought him into close personal contact with the rival factions, and he had felt all the irritation of seeing a tiny Protestant congregation weakened still further by party division.

It is a curious fact that he could not even credit these opponents with sincerity. To Swift the doctrines of the Anglican Church constituted a definite body of revealed truth. (It must be stressed that Swift was always a High Churchman by conviction; thus, Laud was one of his favourite heroes.) Church doctrine stood for absolute reality; hence Dissent, like Free-thinking, could only be a mark of perverseness. It was not part of Swift's creed that there could be different aspects of religious truth. The man who did not sub-scribe to the doctrines of the Established Church was against Christianity—" He that gathereth not with me scattereth ". Accordingly, toleration could form no part of his religious equipment.

Another reason for Swift's bitterness against Dissent was fear—fear of its increase in power until it should overthrow the Church. That fear had run through his own family history. Had not his grandfather vainly given the savings of a lifetime to help to finance King Charles I in the Civil War seventy years previously? Puritanism had triumphed then, and the Swift family still remembered it. What if history should repeat itself?

Swift's fears were perhaps not without justification. The attitude of the Whig party tended towards the strengthening of the Dissenters. And if the Dissenters came into full power, he knew only too well what the Church might expect.

Indeed, he said, he had read above fifty pamphlets

by Presbyterian divines, denying that toleration was allowable and denouncing it as " a rag of popery ". He was quite sure that if the balance of power turned, the Church in its own turn would not be tolerated. And to him the vision of what might happen was unsupportable :—

> " Methinks I should be loath to see my poor titular bishop in partibus, seized on by mistake in the dark for a jesuit; or be forced myself to keep my chaplain disguised like my butler, and steal to prayers in a back room, as my grandfather used in those times, when the Church of England was malignant ".

The particular occasion of this last-quoted tract— to give it its full title, " A Letter from a Member of the House of Commons in England concerning the Sacramental Test "—was the attempt of the Whig party in 1708 to repeal the Test Act.

The Irish clergy, with Swift in the forefront, were on the defensive at once. Almost to a man they attacked the Government. They were quite convinced that the safety and even the existence of their Church depended upon the continuance of the Test Act. This was a regulation which debarred Dissenters from full rights of citizenship, unless they conformed by taking the Sacrament of Holy Communion according to the usage of the Established Church.

Swift made a hard-hitting defence in this pamphlet of 1708. He had the satisfaction of seeing that his side was successful, for the Test Act was not repealed until after his death many years later.

His principal argument throughout was that toleration by Parliament of all sects would inevitably mean

the growth of the Presbyterian party, until it became
strong enough in due course to persecute the Church
itself. We may summarize Swift's position on the
question of the Sacramental Test by quoting these
two queries, taken from a pamphlet of 1732.

> " Whether it be any part of the question at
> this time, which of the two religions is worse,
> Popery or Fanaticism, or not rather which of the
> two (having both the same goodwill) is in the
> hopefullest condition to ruin the Church ? "
> " Whether the sectaries, whenever they come
> to prevail, will not ruin the Church as infallibly
> and effectually as the Papists ? "

With " Popery and Fanaticism ", Agnosticism fell
likewise under the bitter lash of Swift's satire.

We in the twentieth century may criticize his bigotry,
but, to do Swift justice, he did not believe that the
atheists and agnostics of his day were honest in their
attacks on Christianity. Nor did he think it desirable
from a practical point of view to stir up doubt among
simple people who already had an orthodox working
religion.

It is not unlikely that Swift himself had once had
intellectual qualms about Christianity. But if so, he
succeeded in dealing with them. He believed—and
rightly so—that religion is something which goes beyond
the possibility of tangible proof. He accepted with
all his heart the fundamental doctrines of the Church,
not because he could prove them by his own clear
logic, but because in a mysterious way they had become
articles of his own devout personal creed.

In this he differed from the rationalists of his day;
unlike them, he held that logic had its inevitable

limitations. " I am in all opinions to believe according to my own impartial reason ", he wrote. But the significant qualifications followed—" As far as my capacity and opportunities will permit ". And he added this penetrating and revealing criticism : " Violent zeal for truth hath a hundred to one odds to be either petulancy, ambition, or pride ".[1]

The average man displayed a folly only equalled by his impudence in thinking that he could work out for himself the problems of Life and Death, of Heaven and Hell—being indeed no better qualified for thinking than for jumping over the moon.

With these limitations imposed on the scope of reason, Swift could meet his own intellectual difficulties. His own keen mind could penetrate far into the most difficult problems of theology. But he realized that thought could not go the whole way. He saw that the universe is a mysterious one, and that man can ask many questions for which he can never find logical answers. Accordingly Swift was contented to add to his intellectual equipment the article of Faith. With this weapon he could answer his own doubts, and since these doubts were to him a result of the imperfection of human faculties, he felt that they ought not to be voiced in public.

" The want of belief is a defect that ought to be concealed when it cannot be overcome." [1]

Perhaps these doubts tortured him—who knows how tormenting they may have been ? Swift's mind was more than the average under the influence of powers outside his own control. Did he harbour morbid fears that in temptation to doubt he was falling into sin ?

[1] *Thoughts on Religion.*

D

Perhaps so, for we have his own confession and his own self-acquittal :—

> " I am not answerable to God for the doubts that arise in my own breast, since they are the consequence of that reason which he hath planted in me, if I take care to conceal those doubts from others, if I use my best endeavours to subdue them, and if they have no influence on the conduct of my life." [1]

It is not surprising, in view of these sentiments, that Swift hated those who flaunted agnostic and materialistic theories before an ignorant public. Many times, indeed, he made the suggestion that books attacking the Christian Faith should be forbidden by law, for he knew how impressionable and how half-educated the public was. In point of fact, very many people of that day who professed to be free-thinkers were merely gilded illiterates who imagined that it was fashionably advanced to jeer at God.

" Those who are against religion must needs be fools, and therefore we read that, of all animals, God refused the first born of an ass." [2] Swift jotted down this epigram in later years, convinced still that the man in the street was unfit to think for himself, and that he needed a well-regulated religion to keep him upon the narrow path. Almost certainly Swift was right— his most startling statements have a disconcerting way of being true. He would have agreed with Marx that religion is a dope for the masses—but the difference would have been that Swift believed that that religion had also an objective reality and power.

His second great argument against the freethinkers

---

[1] *Thoughts on Religion.*
[2] *Thoughts on Various Subjects.*

was his statement that freedom of thought was claimed as a cloak for that kind of liberty of action which is really licence.

> " The atheists, libertines, despisers of religion and revelation in general, that is to say, all those who usually pass under the name of freethinkers . . . are not so overnice to distinguish between an unlimited liberty of conscience, and an unlimited freedom of opinion." [1]

This view is set out in broad satirical comedy in that most charming of Swift's pamphlets, " The Argument against the Abolishing of Christianity ".

Swift contributed in a comparatively large way to that most popular of eighteenth-century pastimes— writing against the Deists. Apart from incidental references, he undertook two detailed answers to works which he found particularly obnoxious.

In 1706 one Matthew Tindal, an elderly Fellow of All Souls' College, Oxford, produced a book called *The Rights of the Christian Church*. It gained a double distinction : it was burnt by the common hangman, and it was answered by Swift. In the crowded year of 1708 he drafted a " Severe and Scalping " reply. This pamphlet, however, remained unfinished, and it was not published until many years later.

Five years afterwards appeared a more typical example of Swift's power of satire. This was an answer to Anthony Collins' *Discourse on Freethinking, put into plain English by way of Abstract for the Use of the Poor*. Bentley had demolished Collins in a learned treatise which exposed his inadequate scholarship. Hoadly and the quaint William Whiston had joined

---

[1] *Sentiments of a Church of England Man.*

forces to disprove Collins, and this ill-assorted pair gained another kind of ally in Swift.

The Dean's method of attack was to transcribe Collins' book, and to re-publish it in a form which was very like the original, but with a humorous twist which transformed it from a solemnly dull tome into a witty burlesque. Merely by accentuating the arguments of the original, by touching them up, and by putting in the high lights, Swift managed to lead poor Collins' reasoning along devious paths, and eventually to leave him bogged in a morass of absurdity.

It is worth giving one short extract by way of illustration of the method. Collins had attacked the Bible, using as an argument against its value the fact that every religion in the world had its holy book, which it claimed to be true and infallible.

> " Certainly [said Swift] I quite admit what you say. And the only way to tell which of them is true is to read them all."

Then with intense solemnity he set out a scheme whereby Parliament should provide every citizen with a copy of each of these works—about twenty altogether, Vedas, Koran, and the rest—so that the intelligent population of Britain, by the light of pure reason alone, might decide which Bible was true. And naturally, said Swift solemnly, the consequences would be more than Utopian.

> " A great deal of freethinking will at last set us all right, and every one will adhere to the scripture he likes best; by which means religion, peace and wealth, will be for ever secured to her Majesty's realms."

Here we may leave this aspect of Swift's religion—
his intolerance for non-Christian and non-Churchy
sects and factions. It arose, as we have seen, from
two main sources. One was his ingrained Laudian
Churchmanship, which was far enough away from the
extreme Protestant principles of individual judgment
in matters of religion. " The Church to teach, the
Bible to prove", is the motto of that High Church
School to-day. Swift would have agreed heartily
with that sentiment.

The second cause of his intolerance for all varieties
of Deists and Dissenters was his utter lack of belief
in the brain-power of humanity or of its ability to think
for itself.

The key to the whole subject may be found in one
of the briefest and most memorable of all Swift's
arguments :—

> " The bulk of mankind is as well qualified for
> flying as thinking; and if every man thought
> it his duty to think freely, and trouble his neigh-
> bour with his thoughts (which is an essential part
> of Freethinking), it would make wild work of the
> world ".

CHAPTER IV

SWIFT'S SECRET RELIGION

A Religious Estimate—Sides which Repel—" A Nice Man is a Man of Nasty Ideas "—Eighteenth-century Blind Spots —Foreign Missions—Berkeley and Bermuda—Neglect of the Native Irish—Swift's Masked Mysticism—" A Hypocrite Inverted "—" I Hate Lent "—An Evening Prayer— Sick-bed Ministrations—Secret Vespers—What the World Thought—A Cathedral Lampoon—The Revelation of Suffering—Stella's Deathbed—Last Prayers—Swift's God —" God's Mercy is Over all His Works "—An Old Man's Devotions—Swift's Communion Book—The Last Scene.

BEFORE we leave the green plains of Meath and plunge into the whirlpool of Cathedral matters and busy Dublin streets, and before we read Swift's Church pamphlets and watch him fight his bitter war for Irish justice, we must first try to estimate the real quality of Swift's religion.

We shall in these pages see many aspects of Swift's work for his Church—for example, he was a brilliant pamphleteer, a successful intermediary for the remission of the Irish First Fruits, a sincere preacher, an efficient dean, and a diligent slum-pastor.

In this chapter we are concerned with the personal side of Swift's spiritual life. This is a rather different subject from his tangible Church activities. Nevertheless, these latter suggest something of the power of Swift's religion. It is a Christian axiom that " by works is faith made perfect ", and that the quality of a tree is judged by the kind of fruit which it produces. In the spiritual gloom of the eighteenth

44

century the truth of that principle was made only too plain, for with the deadness of the clergy, Church machinery ran down almost to a standstill. This certainly was not the case as regards Swift. His ecclesiastical work was done so energetically and so enthusiastically that it cannot be ascribed (as some critics have done) to a nervous feeling that for conscience sake a man ought to do at least a certain amount of his duty. The minimum duty of an eighteenth-century divine was something remarkably less than the work which Swift did !

Subsequent chapters of this book will deal with Swift's devotional and sacramental life; they will try to show something of his incensed indignation against sin and immorality and infidelity, and they will tell of his stern fight for the dignity of his Church and of its clergy and their ministrations.

When we try to estimate Swift's character, these aspects must be counted for their full value. There have been plenty of writers willing to depict the essential Swift without considering such matters at all. Thus, Rossi and Hone in their recent biography ignore virtually all the materials used in this book, and with the mutilated remnants they have sketched a selfish, vicious monster whom they style " Swift the Egoist ". Not a few other recent writers have done the same thing. A true biography cannot be constructed in this manner.

Admittedly there are sides to Swift's character which repel, so that a superficial reader of, say, his collected works, might well be forgiven for developing a distaste for him. The loathsome dirt of some of his later degenerate pieces is a stumbling-block even to a sympathizer—though they hardly justify the malicious disparagement which his moral character has suffered from so many hostile writers.

How are we to explain Swift's dirty poems and crude allusions? It is not possible just to explain them away by saying, as some indiscriminate admirers have done, that they were merely typical specimens of eighteenth-century humour. That century was crude enough in its wit, but even it was shocked by Swift's coarseness. Nor does it really help Swift's case if we point out, as someone has done, that there was another dirty-minded ecclesiastic at the same period who also wrote nasty poems.

Swift's contemporary and biographer, Dr. Delaney, was nearer the mark when he pointed out that although these writings are filthy, they are not pornographic. Rather than being wantonly suggestive, as for instance Laurence Sterne's work often is, they make vice seem repulsive and loathsome. Swift had an unbearable repugnance for dirt—a disgust so strong that it obsessed him at times. And so these writings appeared, in what may perhaps be described as the retchings of a poisoned mind.

The problem is not an easy one. Professor Trench, in an all-too-brief review of Quintana's Swift (*Ireland To-day*, March 1937), has given the most satisfying of all the solutions. Its short and concise terms may well be quoted here.

(i) "Normality includes all the reticences of decency. Yet hyper-sensibility is unhealthy and tends to insanity. Swift suffered from hyper-sensibility which, unhealthily—or insanely—found the physical disgusting."

(ii) "Reticence means a shunning of aspects of truth. Swift had a passion for truth which meant a resolute rejection of reticences. He will force himself and everyone else to be a ' realist '."

(iii) " Merge these two contradictories, and you have inevitably psychic reaction taking the form of insane indecency."

It will be well to illustrate these clauses with examples. As regards the first—Swift's hyper-sensibility—a good instance is shown by his tone of shocked prudery in which he writes to Stella in the *Journal* on December 11, 1710, to complain of a letter which had disgusted him. It was from Miss Anne Long, and " quite turned my stomach against her; no less than two nasty jests in it, with dashes to suppose them. She is corrupted in that vile town (King's Lynn) with vile conversation." Anne Long was a very average young woman of the eighteenth century— but even her wit was too coarse for Swift's fastidiousness. (So, too, was that of Bolingbroke and St. John, who found the Doctor an uncomfortable table companion, since he would not allow them to spice the dinner conversation either with bad language or with broad jokes.) Fastidiousness became a fetish with him. Dr. Delaney (p. 118) notes as something remarkable Swift's personal cleanliness and his constant bathings and towellings and paring of nails. Eventually fastidiousness turned to revulsion. " A Nice Man is a Man of Nasty Ideas ", wrote Swift in his *Thoughts on Various Subjects.* Unfortunately this was too true in his own case. All normal people have the edges of their sensibilities blunted sufficiently to face the physical without being hurt by it. That is as it should be. Swift's sensibilities were unhealthily keen, and he found the physical and animal side of mankind utterly disgusting. This was a phase of Swift's madness

—not that brain disease which made him die in a stupor in old age—but a madness which consisted in the abnormal development of an emotion.

Secondly, there was Swift's passion for truth, his hatred of shams and hypocrisy, and his denial of reticence. Examples of this are legion—indeed, it is the mark of all his writings. Consider, for example, the motive which made him write the " Meditation on a Broomstick ". There it was his dislike of Boyle's insipidity and lack of genuine feeling. The whole of *Gulliver's Travels* holds the mirror up to nature— Swift makes it a distorting mirror—and in it he urges man to see himself as he really is, a petty, gross, bestial, fantastic animal. The passion for truth is for Swift a white-hot, searing flame, and it forces him to express his thoughts with a lack of constraint which offends against the reticence of a conventionally normal man. This appears notably in some of his early works, such as *The Tale of a Tub* and the *Essay on the Mechanical Operation of the Spirit*. In old age his revolt against reticence grew worse, and after Stella's death some very unpleasant verses appeared.

It is a pity that the results of these two clashing forces in Swift—these later works of insane indecency— were not burnt. They are in fact the offspring of two unhealthily developed facets in Swift's mind. At times these two forces were outside his own control, and the thoughts generated have won an unhappy and over-stressed immortality. For their perpetuation we must blame scavenging, profit-seeking booksellers rather than the man himself. It is certain that Swift was not responsible for their publication.[1]

Yet they have done so much to colour the popular

[1] On this subject see Appendix.

picture of Swift ! To give a proper perspective may
there not be suggested the valiant fight which Swift
himself had to fight against the odds of his own mental
instability? We have little record of it, save what is
hinted at in this chapter. But that the battle was
fought often, and that it was many times won, may be
guessed from the splendid chronicle of all that Swift
did for good.

This discussion on Swift's aberrations has had
to be inserted, and dealt with once for all at an early
stage. The worst that can in fairness be said against
Swift has been said. His moral character, for instance,
was blameless. His work was done conscientiously.
It now remains for this chapter to find Swift's positive
religion.

First of all, we had better notice two eighteenth-
century blind spots—preferment-seeking and self-
sufficiency. Swift was not altogether ahead of his time
(few men are), and two hundred years ago no one
thought it wrong to obtain or to dispense Church
preferment in ways which we should consider unworthy.
Jonathan Swift secured many preferments for others,
working harder for their benefit than for his own.
And it is almost certainly true to say that he himself
looked for promotion far less for financial gain than for
position and power. He regarded himself as a man with
a mission in life, and he felt that his work could be done
more effectively from a high ecclesiastical station than
from a hedge-parish in the bog.

Again, Swift, like the whole body of the Anglican
clergy, rarely thought of the Christian Church as any
wider than a body of English Episcopalians. That
was a blind spot universal two centuries ago. The
idea of Foreign Missions would have struck him as

fantastic if he ever thought of it at all. Half a century after Swift's death a fellow-minister said to William Carey, the apostle of India, " Young man, if God pleases to convert the heathen, He will do it without your help ". That was the current attitude, and in this Swift was of his period. He admired Berkeley's project for founding a university in Bermuda, and he was not unwilling to put in a good word for his friend, but he considered the whole idea quite visionary. During all Swift's Deanship the only money that went overseas was £5 to one Father Athanasius Paulus, for the purpose of releasing Christian captives in Turkey.[1]

This turn of mind serves to explain Swift's lack of interest in converting the native Irish. There was a great opportunity, but Swift, like all the Church of Ireland, was curiously blind to it. Almost the only genuine effort to do anything was made by one John Richardson, who in 1711 attempted to circulate the Scriptures in Irish. Swift was patronizing and gave his assistance half-heartedly. " I am plagued with one Richardson, an Irish Parson, and his project of printing Irish Bibles, etc. to make you Christians in that country ", he wrote to Stella in the *Journal* on April 2, 1711. " I befriended him what I can."

Apparently he imagined that the effective way to obtain mass conversions would be to abolish the Irish language and to suppress the Roman Catholic clergy. " I am deceived if anything has more contributed to prevent the Irish from being tamed than this encouragement of their language, which might be easily abolished, and become a dead one in half an age, with little expense and less trouble." It certainly was not until after his death that Gaelic services were held in St. Patrick's. The very first one recorded was during the Lent of

[1] Proctor's Accounts, 1733.

1758, as an advertisement in *Pue's Occurrences* of February 11 informs us.

With these things must be remembered that the eighteenth-century clergy hid their religion under a cloak of unemotionalism; and it may not be too much to say that behind a frigid mask, behind Swift's unreasoning fear of " fanaticism ", there lay a mysticism more deep and more genuine than even he himself admitted.

Samuel Butler wrote in *Hudibras* of his Puritan Knight Errant :—

> " For his religion, it was fit,
> To match his learning and his wit ".

Of Swift this was very far from being the case. His religion was something very real, but it was hidden away within the depths of his own soul. It was very different in kind from that side of his nature which he chose to show to the world. Because of this reticence in religion, Swift was often judged in religious matters by a lower standard—by this standard of learning and wit. In fact, both were poles apart from the simple and straightforward creed which he believed devoutly and practised sincerely and quietly.

Swift made as little show of religion as possible, because he had an abnormally strong hatred and fear of hypocrisy. His customary public worship in London was attendance at the early Sacrament, because at that service he thought that he would make less parade of piety. " His constant way was to go to early prayers and sacrament, which he thought made him less distinguished in his devotions." [1] He was reticent about his deepest thoughts, and it is remarkable how his correspondence deals almost entirely with mundane

[1] Delaney's *Observations*, p. 31.

and superficial matters, and very rarely indeed touches
on the spiritual side.   In his desire to avoid appearing
hypocritical he developed what was really an affectation
of disclaiming all appearance of piety, lest the reality
of his faith might be questioned.[1]   It had, of course,
the opposite effect, that many people very seriously
did doubt his sincerity.   He became what has been
neatly described as a " hypocrite inverted ".   He
developed a fear even of Church observances like Lent.
" I wish you a merry Lent ", was one of his greetings
to Stella.   He dined off a shoulder of mutton on the
last day of Holy Week, out of sheer defiance, just in
order to show his superiority to hypocrisy.   " I hate
Lent, I hate different diets, and furmity and butter,
and herb porridge; and sour devout faces of people
who only put on religion for seven weeks ", he declared
petulantly in the *Journal* (March 5, 1711—12).

And then, in unwitting contradiction of his rough
show of religious matter-of-factness, he retired to bed
early that same night in order that he might be prepared
for attendance at Holy Communion at eight o'clock
the next morning—Easter Sunday.

He prayed, and he believed devoutly in the power
of prayer.   Very lovely is the spirit of devotion with
which his Evening Prayer is charged : " The coming
into Thy presence, the drawing near unto Thee, is the
only means to be changed ourselves, to become like
Thee in holiness and purity, to be followers of Thee as
Thy dear children ".

Swift's sincerity of belief was recognized by the small
circle of his more intimate acquaintances.   When his
very dear friend Sir Andrew Fountaine was seriously
ill, it was Swift who was summoned to pray at his
bedside, as he told Stella in the *Journal* on February

[1] Delaney's *Observations*, p. 120.

11, 1711. " He has been very ill this week, and sent to me early this morning to have prayers, which, as you know, is the last thing." And Sunday by Sunday, as Sir Andrew became convalescent, Swift came to pray with him. A week later he performed the same office for his Laracor parishioner, " poor Mrs. Wesley ", who was " very much out of order ", instead of going to church. As Archbishop Bernard observed, men and women do not seek such services from their friends, however brilliant or delightful in company, unless they are convinced of their sincerity.[1]

Yet he kept his belief in prayer as discreetly hidden as he could. He did not object to telling his very worldly friend Bolingbroke that he went " every day once to prayers " at St. Patrick's, but in that case he knew that these observances would pass as official prayers, and that no credit for piety could very well attach to him for the performance of his bare duty.[2]

What he did not tell Bolingbroke, nor indeed even Delaney, who was one of the closest friends whom he had during his life in Dublin, was the fact that he said family prayers nightly at home in the Deanery for his servants. So fearful was Swift of giving away his true feelings that actually Delaney spent months living in the Deanery before he stumbled upon the existence of this carefully concealed custom. Yet this habit of prayer was a regular thing at a fixed hour every night, in the Dean's own bedchamber.

> " To which the servants regularly and silently resorted at the time appointed; without any notice from a bell, or audible call of any kind, except the striking of the clock."

[1] Introduction to Ball's *Correspondence*, p. 211.
[2] Letter to Bolingbroke, September 14, 1714.

So noted Dr. Delaney twenty years afterwards.

Delaney sums up this curiously contradictory strain in Swift's character in a way which must be reiterated :—

> " There was no vice in the world he so much abhorred as hypocrisy; and of consequence, nothing he dreaded so much, as to be suspected of it. This naturally made him verge sometimes too much to the other extreme." [1]

It was a trait which could only be known to sympathetic friends. The world probably thought Swift an atheist, as did Archbishop Sharp, who advised Queen Anne that it would never do to make a bishop out of a man who did not even believe in Christianity. That inverted hypocrisy was probably unknown to the majority of his acquaintances, and it was too subtle a psychological trait to be explained to people who did not wish to believe in it. It was much easier to call him an atheist, or as Thackeray did in the *English Humorists*, to laugh poor Delaney's defence to shreds with a little convenient inaccuracy, and to sneer. " There was no need surely, why a Church dignitary should assemble his family privately in a crypt, as if he were afraid of heathen persecution ". [2] It was much easier and more convenient for his enemies to accept the obvious, and, like Jonathan Smedley, to nail up witty verses about the Dean's worldiness upon the Cathedral door.

> " Hard to be plagued with Bible, still,
>   And Prayer Book before thee;
> Hadst thou not wit, to think at will
>   On some diverting story?
>
> " Look down, St. Patrick, look, we pray,
>   On thine own church and steeple;
> Convert thy Dean, on this great day;
>   Or else, God help the people.

---

[1] Delaney's *Observations*, pp. 29 ff.
[2] Thackeray, *The English Humorists*.

> " And now, where'er his deanship dies,
> Upon his tomb be graven;
> A man of God here buried lies,
> Who never thought of Heaven."

Many have been misled by Swift's outward appearances to believe that he was utterly worldly, as has been Sidney Dark, who in his *Five Deans* cited, as Thackeray did, his playful letter advising Gay to take Holy Orders as proof that he had no vocation and no real religion. And indeed it must be accounted a fault with Swift that his contempt of mankind and its opinion was such that he never exerted himself to correct this very obvious estimate.

Was it of himself that he thought when he wrote in his *Thoughts on Various Subjects*, that " Some People take more care to hide their Wisdom than their Folly " ? The sentence sums up his own failing very accurately.

The true religion of the man was only laid bare in moments of utmost extremity. With his friends he was the man of the world, the politician, and the wit. Even to Stella he did not often reveal his deepest thoughts, if we are to judge by the *Journal*. But when the Stella he loved lay dying—that little girl whom he had taught to write, so that her hand became almost a duplicate of his own, that Stella for whom he had bought a Bible and commended her for wanting to read it—then we see for a moment behind the mask of pretence. There is a very wonderful spirit of devotion and of faith in the prayers which he composed for her and which he used at her bedside.

Here is an extract from one of the three which are preserved—they are almost too private and too sacred to dwell on in public :—

> " Lessen, O Lord, we beseech thee, her bodily pains, or give her a double strength of mind to support them. And if thou wilt soon take her to

E

thyself, turn our Thoughts rather upon that Felicity which we hope she shall enjoy, than upon that unspeakable Loss we shall endure. Let her Memory be ever dear unto us; and the Example of her many Virtues, as far as human infirmity will admit, our constant Imitation. Accept, O Lord, these Prayers, poured from the Bottom of our Hearts, in thy Mercy, and for the Merits of our Blessed Saviour. Amen."

One can see in these intimate thoughts something of Swift's trust in God as a God of Love. Dr. Johnson wrote of Swift's prayers a remark which, if it was not spiteful, was entirely misjudged. He said, " The thoughts of death rushed upon him at this time. . . . It seems that his first recourse was to piety." [1]

That is certainly untrue. His revealing *Thoughts on Religion*—one of the few writings which go really deep—speaks of a trust in a God who is merciful and loving. " God's mercy is over all his works," he said, " but divines of all sorts lessen that mercy too much." And it is sure that through all his pain-racked life he did not fear death. He looked on death as a gateway to a fuller and greater life, and a month before Stella's death he could write to a bereaved mother to assure her that this world was but a preparation for a better one, " which you are taught to be certain that so innocent a person is now in possession of; so that she is an immense gainer, and you and her friends the only losers ".[2]

Death held no real terrors for him. " It is impossible ", he wrote, " that any thing so natural, so necessary, and so universal as death, should ever have been designed by providence as an evil to mankind." [3]

[1] Johnson, *Lives of the English Poets.*
[2] Letter to Mrs. Moore, December 7, 1727.
[3] *Thoughts on Religion.*

Perhaps after Stella's death it was what he would have wished for himself. There was an unbearable emptiness in his life when she had gone. There is something infinitely tragic in the way in which he sat down when he heard the news and began to write feverishly his pathetic little catalogue of her virtues, " On the death of Mrs. Johnson ", until his head ached and he could write no more. On the night of the funeral he was too ill to attend, and he moved from his study into another apartment that he might not see the funeral lights in the church.

The last seventeen years of his life were years of loneliness, forgetfulness, and oblivion. During those years he prayed; he prayed still after he became too ill to attend daily service in the Cathedral, and he prayed until he could no longer remember anything of his devotions save " Our Father ". In after years his faithful servant, Richard Brennan, told how he kept on saying that prayer until the very end.[1] It is happy that after two centuries we have been privileged to obtain a glance of that quiet devotional life, so secretly guarded and nurtured. A silent witness remained behind him—a Communion book soiled and thumbed with the daily use of the prayers which he loved.

.   .   .   .   .

And now again we roll back the years to the youth of Swift, and to the days when he was virile and impatient and fired with an impetuous zeal to reform the world. It is the year 1708. He will not be Dean for another five years.

[1] Craik, *Life of Swift*, p. 492.

CHAPTER V

THE FIRST FRUITS

Queen Anne's Bounty—Ireland Appeals—Swift's Mission—
The Whigs Disappoint Him—Home in Laracor—The
Return to London—Tories *versus* Whigs—Harley Secures
the First Fruits—Two Letters which Crossed—Later
Work of the Board of First Fruits—Swift Obtains his
Reward.

THE year 1708 was a notable one for Swift in many
ways. It was one of his most influential periods of
literary activity. His pamphlets on religion were
something new in the art of publicity, and he was
engaged on important work for his own home Church.
During that year the Convocation of Ireland had
appointed him to treat with the Government for the
remission of two small but burdensome taxes on the
Church of Ireland.

Four years previously the clergy of England had received a similar benefit with the foundation of Queen
Anne's Bounty. The Crown then had restored to the
Church all the Papal first fruits and tenths which at
the Reformation had been annexed by Henry VIII.
This money was applied to the augmentation of the
stipends of small livings. The Church of Ireland had
hopes of a similar grant, more especially because the
Irish clergy were considerably poorer than their clerical
brethren in England.

With this object in view, Swift then went to London
to ask for the removal of the " Twentieth Parts "—
a levy of a shilling in the pound on the value of all

JONATHAN SWIFT IN 1708.

From the painting by Charles Jervais in the National Portrait Gallery, Dublin.

Facing p. 59

benefices as they had stood at the Reformation. He also desired that the " First Fruits "—a tax payable by all incumbents upon promotion—should be converted into a fund for purchasing glebes and for building churches. The total sum involved amounted to about £1000 per annum.

For two long years the whole business languished. Promises were made, only to be broken again. At the end of 1708 Lord Pembroke, the outgoing Lord Lieutenant, told Swift that the grant had been sanctioned. For a few weeks it seemed as if Swift had triumphed. But in March 1709 Swift had to write to Archbishop King to admit that the whole thing had collapsed hopelessly. With nothing further in view, Swift returned to the obscurity of his parish in Co. Meath.

For a year and a half, during 1709–10, we find Swift in retirement in Laracor, quietly tending his quicksets and his formal gardens, preaching to his tiny congregation, and living as the simple country parson.

Suddenly, on September 10, 1710, Swift reappeared in London. His arrival was staged at a crucial moment, for his old allies the Whigs were in a critical position. Godolphin and Somers and Halifax made urgent overtures to their former pamphleteer, realizing at last that he was a valuable ally and a dangerous enemy. Lord Somers tried to explain away his neglect of Swift's interests, and the Whig leaders made frantic efforts to show him last-minute favour. It was to no avail, for Swift received all their apologies with frigid politeness and without conviction.

On the 4th of October, Swift was introduced to Harley. A few days afterwards began the elections which were to carry Harley and his Tory party to power. Harley, being an opportunist and a diplomat, received Swift with the greatest goodwill, and promised immediately to arrange for the First Fruits and Twentieths. Swift was plied with hospitality; he was invited to meet St. John and to dine with Harley as a guest of honour. A week after the first introduction —on the 10th of October—Harley promised to see that the whole affair was settled by the following Sunday, and barely a month afterwards Swift was able to write officially to Archbishop King that he had successfully secured the grant.

Meanwhile the Bishops of the Church of Ireland had been studying political conditions, and they had decided that their envoy was far too Whiggish to be of any influence with a Tory Government. Their two official advocates, John Hartestong, Bishop of Ossory, and Thomas Lindsay, Bishop of Killaloe (both paid more than adequately for their labour!), had returned home having accomplished nothing. Accordingly the discouraged Irish Bench decided to make a fresh start, to recall the vicar of Laracor, and to place the business in other hands.

Indeed, they went as far as to send a messenger to take back Swift's papers and to present an address to the Duke of Ormond, asking him to approach the Queen and to induce her to remit the First Fruits.

Archbishop King wrote to Swift to notify him of this decision, and by an accidental stroke of irony worthy of Swift himself, the letter crossed with his own note to the Archbishop telling of his success.

Swift was a strong supporter of the theory of episco-pacy, but he was no lover of Bishops taken individually. Here was the enemy delivered unto his hands! He could now afford to justify himself in more than plain terms.

" I writ a very warm answer to the Archbishop
immediately [he said] and showed my resentments,
as I ought, against the Bishops, only in good
manners, excepting himself. I wonder what they
will say when they hear the thing is done? [1]
They may hang themselves for a parcel of insolent
ungrateful rascals." [2]

The actual patent was drawn up and sealed a couple
of months later. It was dated February 7, 1710–11.
Its terms exonerated the clergy of Ireland from paying
the Twentieth Parts, and it granted to them the First
Fruits, to be held in trust for ever towards purchasing
glebes and building residentiary houses for poor endowed vicars.[3]

Swift deserves more credit from the Church of Ireland
for this piece of work than is generally given to him. The
accumulated trust money thus secured enabled a vast
amount of building to be done in the beginning of the
nineteenth century. Practically every country church
and vicarage to-day owes its existence to a grant or a
loan from the Board of First Fruits. For instance,
both Laracor and Rathbeggan, Swift's own parishes,
secured new nineteenth-century residences and churches
by means of its assistance.

The time now was ripe for Swift to receive his
reward. In politics he was one of the most influential
men in England. He was able to dispense patronage
for others, though for two years preferment eluded him.
He had rendered signal service to his Church. He
might reasonably have expected not less than a bishopric.
But the enmity of the Queen was an insurmountable
barrier in his way. Anne would not consent to allow

---

[1] *Journal to Stella*, November 24, 1710.
[2] *Ibid.*, November 29, 1710.
[3] Nichols, note to *Journal*, February 9, 1711.

Swift on the Bench of Bishops. Harley continued
" mighty kind ", but nothing came of it.   By the spring
of 1713 Swift had become thoroughly impatient, as
indeed most men in his position would have been.
At last the powers that be decided that he could no
longer be left as a mere " hedge parson ".   John
Stearne, the Dean of St. Patrick's, was promoted
to the bishopric of the diocese of Dromore, and by
warrant of April 23, 1713, Swift was appointed to
the vacant Deanery.

CHAPTER VI

THE RELATIONSHIP OF SWIFT'S POLITICS AND RELIGION

From Whig to Tory—*Sentiments of a Church of England Man*— Winning the Laughers—Degradation of the Church— *Argument against Abolishing Christianity*—*What Passed in London*—Status of the Priesthood—Episcopacy— Inferior Irish Bishops and Clergy—*Essay on the Fates of Clergymen*—*Project for the Advancement of Religion.*

WE must now glance back a little way to consider more fully the significance of Swift's change in politics.

In 1710 the Whig party went out of power. As we have seen, Swift began his political career in London as an ally of the Whigs, who were Low Church, or Latitudinarians. When the Tories took office, Swift enlisted with the new party in power. He has often been attacked for his political inconsistency, but it seems clear that his new loyalties were not assumed from any motives of personal gain. The Whigs could never have been entirely congenial associates. In the paramount matter of religion Swift was always a Tory, for the Tories represented the High-Church party, to which he owed allegiance. It is clear that for some years Swift's political attitude was changing, and that his distaste for the Whigs was growing. The Latitudinarian party showed only too plainly that it cared little for the Church, and Swift was quick to mark the contrast between the manner in which they and the Tories had dealt with Church problems. In the matter of the First Fruits, the Whigs had given him scant satisfaction; the Tories carried the reform

63

through.　On the accession of the Tories, the suggestion
for building new churches which Swift had made in
1709 was adopted.　In May 1711 the House of Commons voted a sum of £350,000 for this excellent purpose.
Writing in *The Examiner*, the Tory organ, Swift noted
with satisfaction, how Parliament, in contrast with
its former Whiggish apathy in things spiritual, now
" takes the necessities of the Church into consideration
. . . and amid all the exigencies of a long expensive
war . . . finds a supply for erecting fifty edifices for
the service of God ".[1]

The rift with the Whigs was complete.　Three years
later he wrote of the deanery cat, the pet of the Bishop
of Dromore, that " by her perpetual noise and stink
she must be certainly a Whig ".[2]

Now, to understand the real meaning of Swift's
political inconsistency, it is essential to remember
that throughout all his most active period in politics
his first loyalty was to the Church.　He was a genuine
believer in the Establishment, not on any philosophical
grounds—Swift never troubled to work out the metaphysics of his religion—but from sincere personal
conviction.

Indeed, when this period closed and he had finally
settled in Dublin, he professed to Archbishop King,
sincerely we may believe, that all his share in party
politics had been directed only to the good of religion.
" My friendship I had with the late Ministry, and the
trust they were pleased to repose in me, were chiefly
applied to do all the service to the Church that I was
able ",[3] he said.　This is a very significant passage,
for Swift's truthfulness is undoubted; whatever else

[1] *The Examiner*, No. 42, May 24, 1710.
[2] Letter, October 20, 1714.
[3] Letter, June 17, 1716.

may have been said of him, none of his critics has ever ventured to suggest falsehood as one of his failings.

It was inevitable, then, that his split with the Whigs should have come. The Whig leaders exemplified all that was unsatisfactory in eighteenth-century religion. Lord Wharton was characteristic of the blasphemous type of " Free Thinker " all too common at the time. Hence it became a matter of religious conviction with Swift that he should gravitate to the Tory party.

The foreshadowings of his defection from the Whig party may be seen, too, in that series of pamphlets on the Church which began in 1708, and which produced in quick succession *The Sentiments of a Church of England Man*, the *Letter on the Sacramental Test*, the *Argument against the Abolition of Christianity*, and the *Project for the Advancement of Religion*.

The first named of these papers was an attempt to reconcile a Whig attitude in politics with a High-Church position in religion. Despite the ability of the work— and it is very able indeed; even Dr. Johnson admitted that " it is written with great coolness, moderation, ease, and perspicuity "—it did not please his Whig allies. The tone of all these religious pamphlets did give plenty of cause for their accusation that " he was not Whig enough ". Indeed, when we remember that the Whig party was the stronghold of the various sectaries, the kind of attempt which Swift would make to arrive at a compromise was bound to fail.

He was at first a Whig in politics, though never a bigoted one. But his high regard for the Established Church and his rigid adherence to definite Church teaching made him very different from the average Whig in religion. His churchmanship was unhesitating.

As we have seen, he did not share the Whig fondness
for dissent.   He believed that sects were mischievous,
and he said that new ones should be checked at their
beginning.   Existing sects (he grudgingly admitted,
rather against his will) might be tolerated, but only if
they did not injure the Church.   And so we find him
writing that—

> " Sects in a state seem only tolerated with any
> reason, because they are already spread; and
> because it would not be agreeable with so mild a
> government, or so pure a religion as ours, to use
> violent methods against great numbers of mis-
> taken people. . . . But the greatest advocate of
> general liberty of conscience will allow that they
> ought to be checked in their beginnings."

In these pamphlets of 1708 Swift nails his colours to
the mast and shows his genuine principles.   They
were little to the taste of the Whigs, who had been
working hard all this while to conciliate the Dissenters.
No doubt Swift could have gained promotion if he had
sacrificed his principles and avowed a thorough-going
Whiggish Latitudinarianism.   To his cost, but to his
everlasting credit, he did nothing of the sort.   Rather
he chose the more honourable course, and changed his
politics.   His enemies cried " Turncoat " and wrote
ribald verses about him :—

> " When Wharton reigned, a Whig he was;
> When Pembroke, that's dispute, Sir;
> In Oxford's time, what Oxford pleas'd;
> Non-con, or Jack, or Neuter." [1]

But any discerning churchman must admit that if
Swift was sincere in his personal creed, there was no
other possible course for him to take.

[1] Verses by Smedley, Mason's *St. Patrick's*, p. 269.

The same anti-Whig atmosphere may be felt in his characteristic *Argument against Abolishing Christianity*, also written during 1708. This ingenious tract satirizes amusingly the religious indifference of his day. Swift believed that half the battle was won if he had the laughers on his side. As we have seen, he overdid the method in that youthful volume which had contained *The Tale of a Tub* and the *Essay on the Mechanical Operation of the Spirit*. Here the satire is less outrageous and less obscure, and for that reason it is all the more effective.

It has been the lament of clerics of all ages that religion was never at so low an ebb as during their own period. But it does seem true that Swift had terribly real grounds for attacking the religion of his time. During the eighteenth century the spiritual influence of the Church was at its very lowest. In that century the saintly Bishop Butler had actually refused the Archbishopric of Canterbury on the grounds that he was too old and feeble to attempt the defence of a tottering Church. Church appointments were made with a cynical indifference for spiritual qualifications. Livings were held in plurality everywhere and parishes were left unserved, or the religious offices were held up to contempt by their pastoral work being done by miserably underpaid and under-qualified curates. In Ireland, at any rate, absenteeism was the rule, so that Archbishop King could write that he was ashamed to stay for any length of time in London, it was already so full of Irish Bishops and clergy who lived away from their cures. Swift himself was not above reproach, although he did keep the interests of Laracor in mind, employed the efficient Mr. Warburton as his curate, and gave his parish a good deal of personal attention.

In England adequate church accommodation was as lacking as an adequate ministry. Many country parishes contained no church, or nothing more than a ruined or dilapidated one. In the Forest Deanery of Gloucester in 1750, out of thirty-five churches, twenty-three only professed to have one service on Sunday. The *Journal* of Bishop Nicholson of Carlisle, who ventured to explore his diocese in the beginning of the eighteenth century, is full of entries like these : " The church here is demolished ". " The church is in a very ill state." " The inside of the church was full of water." " The church looked more like a pigsty than ye House of God." Of one church he wrote :—

> " The roof is miserable shattered and broken. Not one pane of glass in any of the windows. No flooring. No seats. No reading desk. They happened to bring a corpse to be buried according to the custom of the place without any service whilst we were there. I desired Mr. Benson, my chaplain, to officiate, but he could only find some few scraps of a Prayer Book and an insufferably torn Bible of the old translation." [1]

It was possible everywhere to find cases as flagrant as that of the parish in England where the sole pastoral care consisted of the erection of a tent on the site of the vanished church for the induction of an absentee rector, in order that he might have a lawful claim to the tithes.

Meanwhile England and Ireland were crying out for the labours of a diligent, devoted body of clergy—but in vain. At the middle of the eighteenth century the Reverend Phillip Skelton, a clergyman on the borders

[1] G. R. Balleine, *History of the Evangelical Party*, pp. 19 and 20.

of Fermanagh and Donegal, was told by one person
of quality that there were two Gods; by another that
there were three. This kind of thing was not excep-
tional—probably it was the rule. Cases innumerable
could be quoted. The writer recently discovered a
document describing the condition of his own County
Tipperary parish in the eighteenth century. The
tithes were wholly lay impropriate. There was no
kind of religious instruction, and seven hundred people
had no more religion than a vague tradition that they
had once been Protestants. " Some believed that
Christ was an Image, others had never even heard
that Venerable Name ", said a contemporary manifesto.
The time was ripe for evangelism, but neither clergy
nor Government cared enough to make any real effort.

Instead of religion there was practical atheism, crime,
immorality, cruelty, and drunkenness. The eighteenth-
century papers are full of the reports of ghastly cases
of sexual crimes. Bull-baiting was a popular sport.
" A mad bull to be dressed up with fireworks "—so
runs one advertisement in a 1730 newspaper. " A
dog to be dressed up with fireworks over him, a bear
to be let loose at the same time, and a cat to be tied to
the Bull's tail ".[1] Bands of wealthy young black-
guards—the " Mohocks "—roamed London streets,
slitting noses. Swift wrote to Stella in the *Journal*,
saying that he would take good care that at any rate
they did not slit his ! Drunkenness was the rule, even
among the statesmen. It was bad in England, but even
worse in Ireland. Berkeley noted that an Irish
squireen, with £100 a year, spent as much on drink as
an English gentleman with £1000. Among the poorer

[1] Quoted by Lecky, *History of England in the Eighteenth
Century*, Vol. I, p. 552.

classes the removal of all restrictions on the sale of
English spirits caused shocking results in the middle
of the eighteenth century. Gin was sold without
restriction from barrows in the streets, and it was
shamelessly hawked from door to door. " Drunk
for a penny, dead drunk for twopence, clean straw
for nothing "—so ran the tempting signs over the gin-
shops. " Should the drinking of this poison be continued at its present height during the next twenty
years ", wrote Fielding in 1751, " there will by that time
be very few of the common people left to drink it." [1]
Even before this date drunkenness was the curse of
the British Isles. Two advertisements taken at
random from the same day's issue of a Dublin journal
are suggestive.[2]

> " To be sold by Pat O'Brien by the Hogshead,
> Dozen or Gallon ".
>
> " Choice old Bordeaux and Graves Claret, French
> White-wine, Lisbon White-wine, dry Mountain,
> neat old Canary, Frontiniack, old Red Port, old
> Hock and other wines ; also neat Contiack Brandy,
> Rum, Holland-Geneva, French Cherry-Brandy,
> right good Orange-Shrub made of pure Rum, and
> choice rough and sweet Cyder at the most reasonable
> Rates for ready money."

That was one side of the picture. In the next
column of the journal appears the second advertisement, which displays the other side.

> " ELIXIR DIVINUM HERM : BEERHAAVE
> or
> The Powerful and Divine Drops of the late in-
> genious Physician Herman Beerhaave, being

[1] Fielding, Pamphlet *On the Late Increase of Robbers*, 1751.
[2] *Pue's Occurrences*, Dublin, July 30, 1743.

the Greatest, and the most comfortable Bitter ever prepared by Mankind; they carry off all Nauseas from the stomach caused by Hard Drinking . . ."

The eighteenth century was an age of sad abuses. In the issue of *Pue's Occurrences* which appeared in Dublin on October 30, 1736, there is a poem which sums up the times. It is entitled " A Short View of some of the World's Contents ", and it reads very like Swift's work—either that, or more probably, the work of one of his disciples.

" A world that's full of Fools and Madmen,
Of over glad and over sad Men,
With a few good but many bad Men.

" So many cheats and close Disguises,
So many down for one that rises,
So many Fops, for one that wise is.

" So many Women, ugly, fine,
Their inside foul, their outside shines,
So many Prelates, few Divines.

" So many of religious Sect
Who quite do mis-expound the Text,
About they know not what perplext.

" So many loose ones and high flying.
Who live as if there was no dying,
Heaven and Hell and all defying.

. . . . .

" A World wherein is plenteous Store
Of foppish rich, ingenious poor,
Neglected, forc'd to beg from Door to Door."

That was the eighteenth-century world that Jonathan Swift looked out upon with agony of soul.

All this kind of indifference and debauchery roused Swift and inflamed that indignant sense of justice which was so characteristic of the man.

The *Argument against the Abolition of Christianity*

F

is an admirable piece of irony on all this deadness in religion. It begins with an apology for a statement as seemingly paradoxical as his opening thesis, that he does not see the absolute necessity of extirpating the Christian religion. For Christianity (that is to say, of course, a nominal Christianity) has certain advantages, strange though the fact may seem. First of all, a nominal religion is a useful butt for people to attack, because if men cannot have a God to revile, they will speak evil of dignities, and they may even abuse the Government. Then, the existence of a body of ten thousand parsons, reduced by the wise regulation of Henry the Eighth to the necessity of a low diet and moderate exercise, ensures a healthy stock for breeding and preserves the nation's health.

Likewise Sunday is a useful day for traders to make up their accounts and lawyers their briefs. The taverns remain open, and it is very convenient to have the churches as places of rendezvous for the gallants and as comfortable places in which to sleep.

While some object that the parsons rail against their pleasures, it is psychologically true that the forbidding of fruit makes it all the sweeter. Indeed, it is to be wished that some other prohibitions were promoted in order to improve the pleasures of the town.

Some scattered notions about a God are not without value among the lower orders; thus God is a useful bogey-man to keep the children in order, and He often furnishes material for conversation in the long winter evenings.

Some people suggest that the abolition of Christianity will unite the various sects—but it must be remembered that if they unite in religion, they will probably divide on something much more dangerous, and instead of fighting about religion, they will most probably attack the laws of the realm. If the quiet of a State can be bought by only flinging men a few ceremonies to devour, it is a purchase no wise man would refuse.

Having refuted gravely the possible objections against Christianity, Swift goes on in a second section to point out some inconveniences arising from the disappearance of an Established Church.

For instance, the wits would be deprived of a good deal of fascinating material for the display of their talents. There would be no parsons to laugh at, and the Free Thinkers would be hard set to find alternative topics to show off their powers. Who would ever have suspected Asgill for a wit, or Toland for a philosopher, if the inexhaustible stock of Christianity had not been at hand to provide them with materials?

Moreover, the abolition of an unobtrusive Established Church, quite inoffensive in itself, would probably encourage Popery and Dissent. As things stand, Christianity provides a harmless outlet for the superstitious instinct of worship which might otherwise seek undesirable channels.

Besides all this, the present quarrel with religion is only because its detractors think that it limits freedom of action. The Free Thinkers try to pull nails out of the fabric of religion, imagining that thereby the whole edifice will fall down, and that they will be allowed to do anything they like. There was a happy instance, he recalled, when a Free Thinker heard that a text brought for proof of the Trinity was differently read in a different manuscript. "Why, if that be as you say", cried the Free Thinker, jumping through a long sorites to its logical conclusion, "I may safely drink on and defy the parson."

It would be better, on the whole, to defer the proposal
to abolish Christianity until the international situation
was more propitious.   We do not want to offend our
allies, who, by the prejudices of their education, are
mostly bigoted Christians.   Nor would we even please
the Turks by so doing.   They would be even more
scandalized at our infidelity than our Christian neighbours, since they are not only strict observers of religious
worship themselves, but, what is worse, they believe
in a God.

To conclude, the crowning argument is that in all
probability the Bank and East India Stock might fall
by as much as one per cent.

> " And since that is fifty times more than ever
> the wisdom of our age thought fit to venture for
> the preservation of Christianity, there is no reason
> we should bear so great a loss merely for the
> sake of destroying it."

Underneath all this fooling was a very real purpose.
Swift was a sincere man, and in an age of corruption
he was a straight and honest one.   He was rapidly
acquiring a strong distaste for the flippancy and
irreligion of his Whig allies; he was sickened by the
levity of the smart set among whom he moved : he
had a contempt for the brutality and ignorance of the
lower orders.   All through life his mind was gnawed
with despair at the grossness of the Yahoo and the
virtual impossibility of raising the standard of the
submerged.   We see this attitude of mind coming
through in bitter works like the *Modest Proposal* or
in the *Directions to Servants*, or in that biting testimonial to a menial written in his old age.

> " Whereas the bearer served me the space of one
> year, during which time he was an idler and a

drunkard, I then discharged him as such; but
how far his having been five years at sea may have
mended his manners, I leave to the penetration of
those who may hereafter choose to employ him." [1]

Another lesser-known work which expresses Swift's
despair for the state of religion—albeit in more playful
vein—is his mock account of *What Passed in London*.

This is a fictitious account of a furore caused by the
self-anointed prophet, William Whiston, the founder
of a freak religious society in 1717 and the author of
innumerable imbecile books on Biblical prophecy.

As late as 1736 this misguided person was still active.
In the Dublin paper, *Pue's Occurrences* of July 10,
1736, an article noted that he had prophesied that in
that year the seventh angel would sound the trumpet
for the Restoration of the Jews; that the tenth part
of Rome would fall; that there would be a great
earthquake; that the affliction of the Church would
cease, and that Antichrist would be destroyed. To
all of which the editor of the journal intelligently
commented :—

> " If these things, or any of them should come
> to pass this Year 1736, of which the Curious will
> take Notice, then surely real regard ought to be
> paid to the Judgements and Sentiments of the
> learned Mr. Whiston : But if none of them shou'd
> come to pass, I am afraid his Expositions and Calcu-
> lations will be deem'd only as the Reveries of a
> visionary Gentleman ".

It so happened, said Swift, that on Tuesday, 13th
of October, Mr. Whiston predicted the coming of the
Comet which was to herald the End of the World.
The Comet was timed to appear at five minutes past

[1] Letter, January 9, 1739–40.

five on Wednesday, and the Judgment before the following Friday night. On the Wednesday morning, at almost the exact moment announced, the Comet did appear! The news spread like wildfire, and by noon on Wednesday the belief was universal that the Day of Judgment was at hand—fixed for Friday.

Promptly religion came into fashion. Thousands gathered in the streets, and at least seventeen went as far as to kneel in prayer (of whom eleven were octogenarian old ladies!). A high financier made restitution by distributing half-crowns among several crazed and half-starved creditors. The pretty little Maids of Honour bathed themselves in order to look their best at the last Judgment. The military chaplains were recalled to their posts—however, the whereabouts of most of them was not known at the time. Three malefactors who were to be hanged on the Monday following expressed satisfaction at the previous arrival of Gabriel's Trump. The Jews on the Stock Exchange reaped great profit by their infidelity. Seven thousand two hundred and forty-five men took their mistresses to wife. Mr. Woolston, the Freethinker ("who writ against the Miracles of our Saviour"), made a public recantation. A good many actors, having very little faith before, now desired to have as much of it as they could, and became Roman Catholics. Many gentlemen hired boats, considering that the middle of the Thames would be the safest place in the universal conflagration. Many other like signs of penitence were shown (detailed by Swift with great gusto), so that by the time Thursday night arrived thousands were seen praying in the public streets.

"In short, one would have thought the whole town had been really and seriously religious.

But what was very remarkable, all the different
persuasions kept by themselves, for as each thought
the other would be damned, not one would join
in prayer with the other."

Then dawned the fateful Friday. Noon came, and
afternoon and evening. And at last, with sunset,
the world was known to be safe.

Now comes the sting of Swift's little parable :—

" The next day, even the common people, as
well as their betters, appeared in their usual state
of indifference. They drank, they whor'd, they
swore, they ly'd, they cheated, they plunder'd,
they gam'd, they quarrell'd, they murder'd. In
short, the world went on in the old channel."

So much for eighteenth-century religion ! The
pity of it was, that Swift's estimate was only too true.

As we admire Swift for his fight for that high standard
which he felt ought to be that of Christian men and
women, so we can almost pity him for that disappointed
ache, that incurable indignation, which the mean reality
caused him. The Church must be the greatest of human
institutions; for him it must be noble and good,
drawing men to lead good lives, teaching honesty and
decency and morality. And it fell so far below the
ideal which he would have, the ideal which, within the
limits of his personality, he himself practised !

This is nowhere clearer than in his attitude towards
the clergy—it was a passionate desire with Swift
that they should be men of dignity and education,
selfless, diligent pastors and worthy descendants of
the apostolic line.

Since Swift was a High Churchman, he believed the
Ministry to be a divinely appointed institution. In
Gulliver's Travels he made his hero describe the Bench

of Bishops as a body of holy persons whose peculiar
business it was to take care of religion; men who were
carefully searched out by the rulers through the whole
nation from the most saintly and learned of the priesthood. They were truly the spiritual fathers of the
clergy and the people.[1] In his sermon on the Martyrdom of King Charles I, Swift expressly stated that
Episcopacy was a divine institution, " which having
been ordained by the apostles themselves, had continued
without interruption in all Christian Churches for above
fifteen hundred years ". Elsewhere, he asked whether
" Episcopacy, which is held by the Church to be a
divine and apostolical institution, be not a fundamental
point of religion, particularly in that essential one of
conferring Holy Orders "? [2]

It is a sad commentary on the way in which reality
fell short of what ought to be, that Gulliver's statement
of the ideal could be an ironical attack on what actually
was.

For the bishops and the clergy, more especially in
Ireland, were a very inferior body. Consider the case
of the Irish prelates of the eighteenth century. Good
and even saintly bishops existed, but they were the
exception rather than the rule. For every one ecclesiastic of the type of Archbishop King—a splendid bishop
—there were half a dozen like Hoadly, or Swift's enemy,
Evans of Meath, who had a bitter contempt for his
Irish clergy, or Primate Stone of Armagh, who had tossed
a coin in his youth to decide whether he would take a
commission in the army or enter Holy Orders. One
or two illustrations will serve to show something of the
condition of the Irish Bench. Only six years before

[1] *Voyage to Brobdingnag*, Chapter VI.
[2] *Queries relating to the Sacramental Test*, 1732.

Swift came to Laracor, Bishop Hackett of Down had been deprived—a bishop who during the twenty-two years of his episcopate had lived in Hammersmith, had openly sold livings to the highest bidders, and had admitted Roman Catholics to Church of Ireland livings by giving them false certificates of subscription.[1] In 1714 Archbishop King wrote of the province of Armagh, which supported eight bishops, including the Primate, that " There has been but one bishop resident at a time in that province for several years. There are now two in it. I can't count the Bishop of Derry resident or any other that only goes there to settle his rents or make a visitation." As a matter of fact, most of the bishops resided in England and their appointments were entirely political ones, made on a basis of whether they would support English policy in Ireland.

Such is the contrast between the stark facts and Swift's ideal of Apostolic Succession in fact as well as in name, that we cannot be surprised at his vigorous enmity towards nearly all the prelates of his day.

He once went so far as to describe Satan as the bishop to whom the rest of the Irish bench were suffragans. He professed to believe that all the new Irish bishops were murdered by footpads on Hounslow Heath on their way to Dublin, and that those same highwaymen stole their robes and patents and usurped the Irish Sees. He said that he would not look into a coach for fear of seeing a bishop. He bade his own Diocesan, Evans of Meath, to remember that he was speaking to a clergyman, and not to a footman.[2]

The same opinion appears time out of number in

[1] Allison Phillips, *History of the Church of Ireland*, Vol. III, p. 168.
[2] Letter, May 22, 1719.

his letters. He described Bishop Ben Hoadly (not unjustly perhaps) as " one whom you would not allow a curate in the smallest of your parishes ",[1] and he said of him that he would be glad at any time to see fifty such bishops hanged.[2]

On another occasion, attacking the bishops for supporting " two abominable Bills for beggaring and enslaving the clergy (which took their birth from Hell) ", he decided to " hold no more commerce with parsons of such prodigious grandeur, who, I feared, in a little time, would expect me to kiss their slipper ".[3]

Strong language, indeed !—but not without justification. Another complaint which Swift constantly aired was the gross nepotism of these English-appointed bishops. With justice he said that this abuse must kill all ambition among the Irish clergy to excel in learning and theology, since these prelates—often obscure clergy without any qualifications of their own other than that of having been chaplains to the governors [4]—drew after them colonies of sons, nephews, cousins, or old college companions, on whom they bestowed the best preferments in their gift, leaving Dublin University qualified clergy with no better prospect than that of being curates or small country vicars for life.[5]

It hurt Swift, too, that these and other causes had reduced the priestly dignity from the high status which it ought to possess. He openly gloried—for the sake of the Church—when a certain clergyman of title took his seat in the House of Lords. He recounted sadly

[1] Letter to Bishop Atterbury, March 24, 1715–16.
[2] Letter to Archbishop King, September 28, 1721.
[3] Letter to Bishop of Clogher, July 1733.
[4] Letter to Earl of Peterborough, April 28, 1726.
[5] Letter to Lord Carteret, July 3, 1725.

how in London he and his man, Patrick, had to separate
a drunken parson from fighting with a sailor. " It
mortified me to see a man in my coat so overtaken ",
he said.[1] Unhappily that failing was not as uncommon
as it should have been. Elsewhere he said that the
sight of a scoundrel in a gown reeling home at midnight (" a sight neither frequent nor miraculous ")
was inclined to give the onlooker a bad opinion of the
whole order of the priesthood, and at the same time
that it would comfort him extremely in his own vices.
Swift's own predecessor at Kilroot, Prebendary Mylne,
had been punished for the same offence and for adultery.[2]

In passing, it may be noted that Swift himself was
thoroughly abstemious. He has left us his own receipt
for sobriety :—

> " Drink little at a time ;
> Put water in your wine ;
> Miss your glass when you can ;
> And go off the first man ".[3]

It was perhaps inevitable that the standard of the
parish clergy in Ireland should be low, for the very
fabric of the Church organization conduced to an
inferior priesthood, just as the policy of the bishops
did. Through the centuries Irish Church endowments
had been pillaged, and the tithes of many benefices
were in lay hands. The incomes of many dioceses
had come down almost to vanishing point. For
instance, during part of the eighteenth century the
average value of the livings in the Diocese of Ossory
had fallen as low as £43 14s.[4] Small as were the values

[1] *Journal to Stella*, May 5, 1711.
[2] Allison Phillips, *History of the Church of Ireland*, Vol. III,
p. 169.
[3] *Journal to Stella*, April 21, 1711.
[4] Bishop Mant, *History of the Church of Ireland*, Vol. I,
p. 663.

of the livings, many of them were served by miserable
curates existing on a fraction of the available income.
Archbishop King gives a picture of the Diocese of
Leighlin which reflects badly on the clergy if it also
explains something of the reason for their worthlessness.
In that diocese, out of 131 parishes, 71 were lay impropriate. Of the remainder, 28 went to the upkeep
of the bishop and the Cathedral dignitaries, leaving
only 32 for the officiating clergy. The whole diocese
was served by only 13 beneficed clergy and 9 curates,
each paid about £30 per annum. Neither Bishop,
Dean, nor Archdeacon resided within the diocesan
boundaries.[1] Under such conditions it was almost
inevitable that the clergy should become demoralized.
Nor indeed is it surprising that Swift should become

> " A clergyman of special note,
> For shunning others of his coat ".

He hated the nervous pretence among clergy of keeping apart from the world, believing that this reduced
their influence. He disapproved of the action of that
bishop who had hoped that none of his clergy attended
The Beggar's Opera.[2] He loathed the pompous emptiness
which commonly passed for sanctity; the dullness
of divines " hot and heavy as a tailor's goose ",[3]
the compliance and time-serving which gained preferment. In the satirical Essay on the Fates of Clergymen
he showed plainly his opinion of the clerics of his
generation.

This brilliant little pamphlet describes the careers

---

[1] Allison Phillips, History of the Church of Ireland, Vol. III,
p. 169.
[2] " A Vindication of Mr. Gay and ' The Beggar's Opera ' "
(Intelligencer, No. 3, 1728).
[3] Archbishop Tenison.

of two men of similar education, but of very different natures and destinies.

Corusodes, the first, was a farmer's son, notable only for a sort of "low discretion". At Oxford he was intolerably well behaved—the kind of man who wore a college gown for five years without tearing it. " He never understood a jest, or had the least conception of wit."

By the good offices of his sister, who was a waiting-woman to a gentleman's family, he gained an entrée to the household. There he fraternized with the servants and developed a talent for gross flattery, both in season and out of it. Then he secured a city lectureship and other minor dignities from his lord— the motive of the latter being not unconnected with an intrigue with Corusodes' waiting-woman sister! He preached constantly, audibly, gravely, and in an ecclesiastical if platitudinous manner. He visited regularly ladies of fashion who had been absent from church, in order that he might chide them and dine with them. He developed a demeanour " formal and starch ". In due course (again through complaisance in the matter of his sister) he achieved the rectorship of a town parish. He employed several curates—paid, naturally, at the lowest rates from the Communion offertory—but he provided them by way of bonus with abundance of good advice. He married a wealthy widow, learned the profitable art of money-lending, never entertained, kept a miserable house, looked down on his inferior clergy, was always complaisant of the doings (virtuous or otherwise) of persons and parties in power, was notable for short, inoffensive sermons in his turns at court, proved himself a good latitudinarian by writing against episcopacy and by condoning dissent—in fact, he crawled and bowed and toadied until he obtained the due reward of a mitre.

> " Endued with all these accomplishments, we leave him in the full career of success, mounting fast towards the top of the ladder ecclesiastical, which he has a fair probability to reach; without the merit of one single virtue, moderately stocked with the least valuable parts of erudition, utterly devoid of all taste, judgment or genius ".

So much for a successful ecclesiastic. Now comes the picture of Eugenio, a clergyman who had not been endowed by nature with those gifts which were calculated to make him rise. He was a scholar, a gentleman, and a wit, and accordingly he was not popular with his more sedate clerical superiors. His first appointment was as reader in a parish church at £20 a year. There he was commended by poetical friends to sundry great persons as a young man deserving of encouragement— being, in fact, a genuine scholar and an excellent preacher, if a little too original to be entirely acceptable.

Unhappily he never gained the promised preferment, always being forestalled by " vigilant dunces " who were waiting to pounce on any promotion going. However, everyone said that " it was a thousand pities that something could not be done for poor Mr. Eugenio ".

Eventually, to cut a long story short, he despaired of any promotion whatsoever and accepted a curacy in Derbyshire at £30 a year—

> " and when he was five and forty had the great felicity to be preferred by a friend of his father's to a vicarage worth annually sixty pounds, in the most desert parts of Lincolnshire; where, his spirit quite sunk with those reflections that solitude

and disappointments bring, he married a farmer's widow, and is still alive, utterly undistinguished and forgotten; only some of the neighbours have accidentally heard, that he had been a notable man in his youth ".

These pamphlets of Swift's make depressing reading, consisting as they do of an expression of the failure of the eighteenth-century Church to fulfil its mission. Apart from their inimitable manner, they are no more than the conventional complaints that religion had gone to pieces. And Swift, as a churchman, might have been less noteworthy if his pen had produced nothing more constructive than mere railing, however brilliant the satire. Lesser minds than Swift's have effectively castigated the conditions of the world around them.

But, to his credit, he made a real effort to find a cure for the irreligion of his day. It was not within his nature to achieve the solution of a Wesley and lead a revival which was to set the heart of England aflame. Viewed in the light of Wesley's enthusiasm, Swift's suggestions of some twenty-nine years earlier seem pale and thin. But at least they were sincere, and they were based upon a real conviction. Those critics of Swift who find in his *Project for the Advancement of Religion* a mere sop to respectability are grievously mistaken. Swift never cared enough for the conventions to misuse his pen in this way.

Unlike almost all other of his Church treatises, Swift here abandons the method of confounding his adversaries by ridicule. Accordingly, the *Project* is among the less entertaining of his works—for that reason, perhaps, it has been undeservedly neglected.

It opens with the surprising statement that there is an easy and obvious method available for raising faith and morals to as high a level as is possible for the average man.

Before letting us into the secret, Swift details the corruption of the age. He tells us that hardly one man in a hundred displays any principle of religion. The lower orders in the cities and in the ranks of the army are apparent infidels, if not actually avowed ones. Men no longer try to hide, or even to palliate, their vices, brazenly admitting charges of drunkenness, immorality, and blasphemy. Women of tainted reputation are received into society. The disease of gambling is rife. Trade is dishonest. The law is riddled with corruption and injustice. Places are sought and given by means of bribery and nepotism. The clergy are ignorant, mean, and servile; their young members are opinionated and pert, and the whole order is contemptible.

Such was Swift's indictment of his age. But damning as it was, he found hope of a remedy—surprisingly enough—in the Crown. This remedy was not to be had merely by the good example of a monarch—the reign of Queen Anne showed plainly enough that the inert, if genuine virtue of a sovereign effected nothing. No—the Crown must make it in every man's interest to cultivate religion and morality. For instance, he asks whether the Queen's domestic staff might not be bound by royal command to attend church and Communion regularly, to avoid swearing, profanity, and open irreligion, and to preserve at least the appearance of temperance and chastity. Might it not be made clear that great officers of State retained favour only so long as they were morally of good behaviour? Why should the bishops not work with the Queen to see that these conditions were observed? Could not

Government officials be obliged to take an oath parallel to that which is taken against simony by the clergy? If these regulations were carefully adhered to, there could be no doubt that morality and religion would become fashionable Court virtues. Undoubtedly the influence from above would filter downwards throughout the nation, purifying the life of all classes of society.

To Swift's credit, it must be said that his scheme was much more practical than it must have seemed to his contemporaries, or even to Sir Walter Scott, who commented on it more than a century later in his great collected edition of Swift's works. Scott wrote, " The idea of a religious administration and Court borders on the visionary ", but, then, he wrote in the corrupt days of the Regency. Victorian England, with its purified Court and its solid, industrious citizens who took as their pattern the Queen and the Prince Consort, demonstrated adequately that there was sound judgment in Swift's thesis. To some extent it is true that even religion and morality are creatures of habit, and a religion which begins merely as hypocrisy may become genuine with time.

This is the central idea of the *Project*, and from here it continues for several pages in a rather rambling manner, throwing out various suggestions as it goes along. Some of these are worth noting as illustrations of Swift's own ethical ideas.

Censors and itinerant commissions of morals should be appointed by the Government. (Certainly the least likely to be tolerated of all Swift's schemes !)

The fashionable Army and Court vices of swearing, drinking, and gambling could be made scandalous if frowned upon by the Crown, and if they involved

G

loss of favour or employment, they must inevitably disappear.

> " How ready therefore would most men be to step into paths of virtue and piety, if they infallibly led to favour and fortune ! "

The Universities and the Inns of Court should be reformed, and the discipline made more strict ; drinking should be forbidden—as well as smoking !

The clergy should mingle with the world, and they should exert themselves individually to become social assets—in short, they ought to try to become popular with the laity. For, as Swift wisely observes, men must be induced to love and esteem their clergy, before they can be brought to care for religion. (This ought not to be, of course, but in practice it nearly always is so. At any rate the converse is true—how many people leave their church because they dislike the parson ?) If the clergy would cease to be a clique apart, and if they had the courage to venture among ordinary men, rather than to hide under a cloak of nervous clerical aloofness, they could become a great force for good. To Swift's mind this latter pose of sanctified apartness is " just as reasonable as if the physicians should agree to spend their time in visiting one another, or their several apothecaries, and leave their patients to shift for themselves ".

The stage next comes in for Swift's criticism. At the beginning of the eighteenth century it had passed through a thoroughly degenerate period. Might it not be reformed? asks Swift. Might it not become " a very innocent and useful diversion " if suitable censors were appointed with power to strike out offensive passages? Thus Swift anticipates the present office of the Lord Chamberlain !

It might be said, remarks Swift, that these methods of advancing religion would lead to hypocrisy. That was true—but if only one man in twenty were to be brought to true piety by such methods, and the other nineteen remained hypocrites, the advantage would still be great, for hypocrisy is more eligible than open infidelity and vice. And if vices became dangerous to commit, most men would abandon them out of mere weariness. Indeed, the practice of mock piety would often bring the real thing in its train.

> " I believe it is often with religion as it is with love; which by much dissembling, at last grows real."

Three other practical suggestions follow, among a good deal of general discussion of the vices of the age.

First, that by law all taverns and alehouses should close at midnight; that women should be forbidden to enter them at any time; that the quantity of liquor allowed to each tavern habitué should be rationed, and that an intoxicated person should not be served with drink. Nearly all sections of this suggestion have since been put into the statute books.

Secondly, that there should be a censorship of books, and that in particular books which attacked the great Christian doctrines should be suppressed. The censorship of literature is a controversial question, but it is interesting to note that it has lately been adopted in Swift's native land, though not on exactly the same lines as he suggested.

Thirdly, that in the towns more churches should be built. Often a single minister with one or two " sorry curates " had to minister to above twenty thousand people. It was this paragraph which gave the first impetus to the fund, in the Earl of Oxford's ministry, for building fifty new churches in London.

Perhaps enough has been said to give a brief idea of the nature of Swift's religious writings, and, what is more important, to portray the man himself in his earlier years.

His own Church of Ireland has learned to see him as a man who was not only great, but also good. He was, especially, an indefatigable worker for his Church— almost a solitary light in a century of religious gloom and apathy and indifference. He had his faults. Pain and that terrible righteous anger—the " *saeva indignatio* " of his epitaph—soured his temper in later years; his sense of decorum was a curiously varying quality; his intolerance in religion and his flint-like lack of toleration for the sinner and the fool were often repulsive. But he was honest, and according to his lights he served his God with every weapon he possessed, for he thought of his ministerial calling as a position with an absolute obligation for service. In his *Thoughts on Religion* he stated his personal conviction:—

> " I look upon myself, in the capacity of a clergyman, to be one appointed by providence for defending a post assigned to me, and for gaining over as many enemies as I can ".

JONATHAN SWIFT IN 1738.
From the painting by Francis Bindon in the National Portrait Gallery,
Dublin.

[Facing p. 91

CHAPTER VII

THE DEAN OF ST. PATRICK'S

JUNE 1713 saw Swift installed in Dublin, Dean of a
massive and dilapidated Gothic cathedral, master of a
gloomy, rambling deanery, and ruler of an independent
neighbourhood, the liberty of the Dean of St. Patrick's.
" I am lord Mayor of one hundred and twenty houses ",
he wrote.   He was still a comparatively young man of
forty-six, strong, a born ruler, intolerant of fools
and knaves ; a character who could be loved by those
who knew him intimately, but who was cordially
hated by any of those foolhardy people who dared to
cross him.

The well-known portrait by Charles Jervais [1] shows
the man in his prime.   There is an air of supreme
confidence in the face—it could be irritating to anyone
who did not know the strength and capacity which

[1] See p. 59.

91

justified it. The eyes under their heavy black brows are magnetic and compelling. A classically minded biographer described him as sitting in his Chapter-house like Jupiter in the Assembly of the Gods,[1] and at first his venerable assembly of sedate colleagues must have found him uncomfortably galvanic. But there is something in the gently humorous lift of his mouth which reveals another side of his character and which explains why he gained the dog-like devotion and love of men like Delaney and Worrall, and why these and the other members of his Chapter became so united in a loyalty to their chairman which lasted for more than thirty years.

The Deanship of St. Patrick's was no easy task. It might have been simple for a complaisant dean, for one tolerant of carelessness, willing to allow old abuses to continue, and contented to adopt a policy of *laissez-faire*. But not for Swift. He was too honest to allow himself to drift.

Nor was his new post altogether pleasant in a personal way. His political record left plenty of room for wilful misunderstanding and even for genuine misunder-standing too. The memory of the grotesque scurrilities of Peter, Jack, and Martin left an ugly taste in the mouths of many who might otherwise have wished him well. In 1714 the Tory party collapsed, leaving him in a hopelessly bad political position in a Whig world. The scum of Dublin hissed him in the streets, and Whig squireens insulted him to his face. No, Ireland was not particularly attractive. As well as every other difficulty, there were money difficulties to be faced. His house and fees had cost him £1000, and the death of Queen Anne dissipated any hopes he had been given of Government assistance. If he

[1] Lord Orrery.

was the richest man in Dublin who managed without
a coach and horses, he was also the poorest who had his
meals off plate.   He lived with a skeleton staff in a
corner of Bishop Stearne's ugly, inconvenient barrack
of a Deanery, surrounded by the most noisome slums
of the city.   His neighbours were the weavers and the
beggars of Dublin, a hostile, alien rabble living in a
warren of dirty streets periodically flooded by the River
Poddle.   And he had to contend with a distrustful
Chapter of jealous fogeys, and with the suspicions of an
archbishop who cared not at all for an over-independent
Dean of St. Patrick's.

The initial difficulties were enough to make any man
lose heart.   The typical eighteenth-century divine
would have retired to Bath and would have sedulously
tried to forget everything about his position except
the dignity and the emoluments.   But Swift had the
misfortune to be a zealous dean.

There is little wonder that at times Swift was de-
pressed.   No wonder there were times when he gladly
retired to the cherry-trees of Laracor and to the rustic
solidity of his little church and the amusing oddities
of poor Joe Beaumont !   No wonder that he sometimes
cried out that he loved his thatched cabin in the Irish
bog better than the ugly barrack that they told him
was his possession !

Critics of Swift—and they are many—have made
great capital of his moments of depression.   They all
have quoted his outburst about dying in a rage like a
rat in a trap, and his verses of October 1713, when he
cried :—

> " My state of health none care to learn,
> My life is here no soul's concern,
> And those with whom I now converse,
> Without a tear will tend my hearse ".

These and many similar items have been used to colour
the picture of a man who looked on his career in Ireland
as an exile as bitter as that of any Russian Grand Duke
in the Siberian salt-mines.

This emphasis is undoubtedly false. These black
periods were intermittent, and they corresponded
with the miserable ailment from which he suffered
throughout his life.

Sir William Wilde has shown clearly the nature
and the effects of Swift's complaint. He suffered
from youth from " Labyrinthine vertigo ", a disease
of the inner ear, which produced torments of giddiness,
sickness, deafness, and roaring in the ears.[1] Attacks
were frequent and agonizing, and the trouble became
more permanent in later life. What it meant is
shown by frequent entries in his journal and his note-
books.

> " Horribly sick. . . . Much better, thank God
> and M.D.'s prayers. . . . Small giddy fit and
> swimming in the head. M.D.[2] and God help me.
> . . . Terrible fit. God knows what may be the
> event. . . ."

Worse than the throbbing sickness was the terrible
anxiety of what it might lead to. All his life he dreaded
madness. In 1717 he said to Young the author of *Night
Thoughts* " I shall be like that tree ; I shall die at the
top ". In pathetic sympathy

> " He gave what little wealth he had,
>   To build a home for fools and mad ",

the present St. Patrick's Hospital in Dublin. He was a
member of the committee of the London Bedlam.

---

[1] Wilde, *The Closing Years of Dean Swift's Life*, 1849.
[2] M.D.—*i.e.*, Stella.

Eventually complete paralysis of the brain came (as distinct from lunacy; Swift was never mad in the popular sense of the word). The last five years of his life were a tragic blank.

This serves to explain much of those dark periods of melancholy and those savage outbursts of temper which have been given such prominence in his biographies.

Allied probably with his disease was a partial paralysis of one side. A recently discovered portrait of Swift [1] shows the left side of his mouth puckered up tightly; his left hand was weak and tremulous,[2] his left ear was deaf. And at the end his left eye swelled up in horrible agony.

So much for poor Swift's handicaps. It is infinitely sad to know that to-day, as a Dublin surgeon recently claimed, ten minutes under an anæsthetic and a small operation could have relieved him.

Mercifully there were intervals, and long intervals, of freedom from pain. And in these intervals he worked zealously as Dean of his Cathedral, pastor of his parish, and governor of his district.

It is very remarkable how this fact has been overlooked. Critics have asked how Swift occupied himself in the intervals between his writings. His entire literary output was a comparatively small one. The crowded hours of the Drapier controversy occupied only a tiny fragment of his thirty-two years of deanship.

However did he fill in his time? ask his critics. The obvious answer is the one which seems to have been very generally ignored. Being a supremely honest man (as well as a sincere churchman), he did the work

---

[1] Now in St. Patrick's Hospital, Dublin.
[2] *Journal to Stella*, May 10, 1712.

for which he had been ordained, and for which he drew his salary. He was pre-eminently Dean of St. Patrick's, and perhaps the best dean the ancient Cathedral ever possessed. After two centuries the ghost of Swift still haunts St. Patrick's; no discerning visitor can miss feeling his presence there. Scores of deans have come and gone, but one only has left his mark in this peculiar way. It is impossible that such a legacy, such an all-pervasive atmosphere, could have been left by one who did not care deeply. Swift's work as Dean was the least spectacular part of his career, but for him it became the most important.

Swift threw himself into his new work energetically and at once. The old vicars and clergy who had lapsed into lazy ways were mercilessly roused. The Cathedral staff was jerked into life. Those who had expected to sleep peacefully under a negligent dean were disappointed. There would no longer be sinecures in the service of the Dean of St. Patrick's. He would not tolerate his Cathedral being anything less than an example to the whole Church of Ireland.

" I hear they think me a smart Dean and that I am doing good ", he wrote to his friend Chetwode. His feeling was that if a man could not mend the public he should " mend old shoes, if he can do no better ". Therefore he was resolved to do all the good possible in his little sphere.[1]

And it is quite true that he did. Delaney, who was a member of his Chapter, and practically our only contemporary authority, gives a very high account of Swift's work. He remarks that his care for his Deanery and Cathedral, together with its organization, finances, and services, occupied Swift's constant

[1] Letter, January 3, 1715.

energies.[1] His account of Swift's pastoral and charitable work is so full and so interesting that it must be reserved for another chapter.

Almost his first act was to reorganize the services. Up to 1713 St. Patrick's had been working in an old, slipshod style with the bare minimum of Sunday services. Swift promptly extended the service list. He added a Sunday afternoon Evensong with sermon, ordering " that the members of this Church, each in their turn . . . do preach in the afternoon or every Sunday in the year except Lent Sundays in the aforesaid church and to commence on Easter Sunday next ". [2] He disciplined the choir, kept his preachers up to standard by criticism and advice, and himself attended daily service at 9 a.m. and often at 3 p.m. unless prevented by sickness.[3] Gradually the spirit of the Cathedral improved, and congregations increased. One thousand people came to be the usual attendance on the fifth Sunday, when Swift preached.

Perhaps most satisfactory of all was his restoration of the weekly Communion. St. Patrick's was the only church in Dublin where this practice prevailed in his time,[4] and it was still so in 1820.[5] In 1717 Swift inaugurated the rule that two of the senior dignitaries should always assist the Dean at the Christmas morning celebration.[6]

A happy, though to most readers an unfamiliar picture of Swift, is given by two of his friends who attended that service. One was Delaney; he says :—

---

[1] Delaney's *Observations*, p. 69.
[2] Chapter Minutes, January, 1714.
[3] Mason, *St. Patrick's*, p. 420.
[4] Delaney's *Observations*, p. 32.
[5] McGregor, *Guide Book to Dublin*, 1820.
[6] Chapter Minutes, January 13, 1717.

" It is most certain that he constantly attended
that Holy Office; consecrated and administered
the Sacrament in person. Nor do I believe that
he ever once failed to do so when it was in his
power. . . ." [1]

The other picture is that given by Swift's amusing
little authoress friend, Mrs. Pilkington; in her
Memoirs :—

" As the Communion is administered every
Sunday in this antique church . . . I was charmed
to see with what a becomng piety the Dean
performed that solemn service; which he had so
much at heart that he wanted not the assistance
of the liturgy, but went quite through it without
ever looking at the Prayer Book. Indeed, another
part of his behaviour on this occasion was censured
by some as savouring of Popery, which was that
he bowed to the Holy Table; however, this
circumstance may vindicate him from the wicked
aspersion of being deemed an unbeliever, since
'tis plain he had the utmost reverence for the
Eucharist."

These two witnesses throw a rather new light on
Swift's devotional life, being perhaps the only two who
have not ignored this side of his character. Delaney
especially is determined to make clear Swift's religious
sincerity, and as a friend and fellow-member of the
Cathedral staff, his evidence must be given full value.
Here is what he says :—

" As to his religion, I think verily, that I myself
have observed many strong indications and
proofs of his sincerity in it, besides those now
mentioned. His saying grace both before and
after meat was very remarkable. It was always

[1] Delaney's *Observations*, p. 32.

in the fewest words that could be uttered on the
occasion, but with an emphasis and fervour which
everyone around him saw, and felt; and with his
hands clasped into one another, and lifted up to his
breast, but never higher." [1]

The fascinating Proctor's Receipt Books in the
Cathedral archives illustrate Swift's career all through
his thirty-two years of deanship—we shall meet them
constantly in these chapters.

And here, as usual, they are enlightening—this time
to confirm the centrality of the Holy Communion as
the great Church service for Swift. Four years after
his installation, when the number of weekly com-
municants began to grow, he purchased a large silver
chalice for the use of the Cathedral.[2] Perhaps it is
significant of the man, too, that his gift to Gooderich
Church, the parish of his royalist grandfather, should
be a cocoanut Communion Cup mounted with silver
which had once been used by that fine old " malignant "
clergyman in King Charles' days.[3]

It did not take long for even outsiders to realize
that a new atmosphere was growing up in St. Patrick's
Cathedral. Only six months after installation Mr.
Justice Nutley wrote appreciatively, noting Swift's
" just intention of bettering the economy of your church,
and mending the beauty and harmony of the service
to be performed in it ".[4]

Gradually decency and order revived. But the
changes did not come altogether peacefully. All
reforms meet with opposition, and Swift had more than

[1] Delaney's *Observations*, p. 29.
[2] Proctor's Accounts, September 25, 1719.
[3] Lecture by Bernard, February 16, 1906.
[4] Letter, November 5, 1713.

one conflict before the confidence of his colleagues was gained.

First of all there was trouble with Christ Church Cathedral. This church had precedence over St. Patrick's; and the two churches were bound together in certain traditional ways. Thus, the Chapter of St. Patrick's were expected to preach in their turn at Christ Church, under penalty of a heavy fine.

But Christ Church had degenerated in the seventeenth and eighteenth centuries. For some years its administration had been unsatisfactory. Much of its fabric was used for secular purposes; there were shops in the crypt and part of its precincts were used as the law courts of Dublin.

Swift promptly relieved his clergy from the responsibility of having any connection whatever with Christ Church. In December 1714 he repealed the penalty for not preaching there when required to do so.[1]

It certainly does not sound an over-brotherly act towards his fellow-Dean, but Swift's action was in line with the subsequent opinion of as fine a churchman as Archbishop King, who wrote of the plight of Christ Church, its own " clergy having withdrawn themselves from preaching in their Church, which they formerly did by turns both on Sundays and holidays; and the nobility and gentry absenting themselves, because they did not see that decency in the service of God and edification in the preaching which they used to have ".[2]

The difference between the decent care with which St. Patrick's was administered and the slovenly negligence of Christ Church at the same period is striking. And the credit must go to Swift. When he had been

[1] Chapter Acts, 1714.
[2] Letter to the Archbishop of Canterbury, May 23, 1724.

in office for eleven years and had effected most of his improvements, Archbishop King could appreciate the notable difference between the two foundations. The archbishop complained of the Dean and Chapter of Christ Church, " who squander away their economy; have turned their chapter-house into a toy shop, their vaults into wine cellars; and allowed a room in the body of their church, formerly for a grand jury room, and now for a robe room for the judges; and are greatly chagrined at my getting two or three churches built and consecrated in the parishes belonging to their body, which were formerly neglected, as several others still are; their cathedral is in a pitiful condition; and though St. Patrick's has not half the oeconomy that Christ Church has yet it is much better beautified, and great sums of money laid out on it." [1]

Swift might well be proud of such a sincere testimonial from his metropolitan Bishop.

During the first five years there were other troubles to be faced. Not only had Swift to fight his way with the dignitaries of Christ Church, but these years were darkened (as we shall see subsequently) by struggles with the Vicars Choral, and also with the members of his own Cathedral Chapter.

What the real reason was for this latter disagreement we cannot tell. The machinations of Archbishop King and Chancellor Theophilus Bolton, afterwards Archbishop of Tuam, certainly assisted in causing trouble. Probably, too, some of it arose from dislike for Swift's discredited Tory politics. (In 1714 he had been pelted in the streets as a Jacobite.) Revolt against his stern and drastic discipline was another cause. The im-

---

[5] Letter to Annesley, February 4, 1724; Mant, Vol. II, pp. 401 ff.

mediate occasion for the outbreak was the exercise of the Dean's veto. Swift claimed the power to annul the proceedings of the majority of the Chapter by virtue of his prerogative as Dean. His Chapter members opposed him firmly. In March 1716 Swift wrote to Bishop Atterbury, asking for his advice, and explaining his difficult position.

> " I am here [he wrote] at the head of three and twenty dignitaries and prebendaries, of which the major part, differing from me in principle, have taken a fancy to oppose me on all occasions in the Chapter House."

It was an organized opposition, not confined only to the technicalities of a Dean's negative. Thus in 1715 a crisis arose over the election of a proctor—the official responsible for the Cathedral finances. On March 24 Swift's proposed candidate was rejected, and when he put his own name forward he was defeated by eight votes to six. It was not until a further meeting a week later that agreement was reached.

Happily the Chapter soon discovered that they were dealing neither with a knave nor a fool, nor with a man who could be intimidated. They found that discretion was the wiser policy, and gradually discretion warmed into affection. They came to realize, as Dr. Johnson said, " that between prudence and integrity he was seldom in the wrong; and that when he was in the right his spirit did not easily yield to opposition ".[1] Very soon *Vox Decani* became *Vox Dei* in the Chapter-house.[2]

Twenty-five years after his appointment we find a tangible token of the regard in which his colleagues

[1] Johnson, *Lives of the English Poets, Swift.*
[2] Orrery, *Remarks.*

held him. By unanimous vote they decided to have his portrait painted at their expense.

This work was done by the celebrated artist Francis Bindon. The full-length portrait still hangs in the Deanery—it was placed there by the Chapter to preserve it from injury, as the Chapter-house was intolerably damp owing to the floods and morasses of the Poddle, which soaked through the foundations of the Cathedral. The Proctor's Accounts preserve Bindon's signature on the original receipt.

> " Received from ye Rev. Dean & Chapter, etc., ye sum of thirty six pounds sixteen shill. sterl. in full for painting a picture by order of Chapter, of Dr. Swift ye present Dean of St. Pat., both in respect to him, & also to preserve the memory of his good Services done for the Church of Ireland. Recd. on ye 7th of March 1738.   Fran. Bindon."

It was a happy tribute after twenty-five years of faithful service as Dean of St. Patrick's. The picture itself shows Swift in gown and bands, holding in his hand a scroll inscribed, " Q. Anne's Letters Patent of the First Fruits etc. for the Poor Clergy of Ireland ". Through a window is depicted the west front of his well-loved Cathedral. But the most striking thing of all is the face of the man himself. It is a strange contrast to that virile, self-confident, arrogant Swift so vividly given to us by Jervais's earlier portrait. Here we can recognize the same full, humorous lips, but the face and the eyes are those of a man who has grown tired and heavy and who has lost his fire. He was still making a brave show before the world—but suffering and pain and old age had left their marks. Stella was ten years dead. Swift himself was over seventy years of age.[1]

[1] See p. 91.

H

When Swift died seven years later, these two portraits
were given broadcast to a sorrowing Dublin.   We find
in *Faulkiner's Journal*, in the issue immediately after
the notice of the Dean's death, this advertisement :—

> " Just published and sold by the printer hereof,
> price 13*d*. each, a very fine engravèd print of the
> Rev. Dr. Swift, D.S.P.D., taken from the original
> Picture painted by Mr. Gervais; and the other a
> Metzotinto taken from the fine original Portrait
> in the Deanery House in Kevin Street, which
> Picture was painted by Mr. Bindon at the expense
> of the Chapter, and is universally allowed by all
> the Friends and Acquaintances of the Dean to be
> the most exact Likeness that ever was taken ".

By this time Swift's work was all but over.   But
during those twenty-five years he had done wonderful
things for his Cathedral.   The Chapter Acts and
Proctor's Accounts are full of hints as to the importance
of his labours.

Here is an appreciation written by one of his contemporaries :—

> " His attention to the repairs of his Cathedral
> was very remarkable; and, I believe, it will be
> found, upon enquiry, that greater sums have been
> applied to the solid support, preservation and
> ornament of that cathedral, in his time, than in any
> preceding period, from its building." [1]

.   .   .   .   .

Fortunately Swift appreciated his old Gothic church
and its historical associations.   Such appreciation
was not altogether common in the eighteenth century.
The treatment of many fine old Gothic churches was

[1] Delaney's *Observations*, p. 136.

ST. PATRICK'S CATHEDRAL IN 1739.

unforgivable, witness the despoiling of Cashel in 1763 by an archbishop who disliked the steep ascent of the Rock, and the demolition ten years later of Waterford Cathedral, a sister church to Christ Church, Dublin. Even Wren declared that these sort of cathedrals were " vast and gigantic buildings indeed, but not worthy the name of architecture ".[1] Swift could see the beauty of Gothic, and a fellow-enthusiast, Theophilus Bolton, invited him down to give his expert opinion about the restoration of Cashel, and to see King Cormac's Chapel, " built beyond controversy above eight hundred years ago ". Bolton intended to lay out £1000 to preserve the old church, and he wrote, " I am sure you would be of service to posterity if you assisted me in the doing it ".[2] Obviously the reputation of Swift's work in Dublin had travelled south.

We can get a good idea of the external appearance of St. Patrick's from a contemporary engraving in Harris's edition of Ware.[3] Minot's great battlemented tower stood at the south-west corner. The Lady Chapel at the east end was used as a church for the French congregation. The north transept served as the parish church of St. Nicholas Without. To the south transept Swift had transferred the Chapter-house in 1730. In another building on the south side of the nave was the Consistory Court, transferred here in 1724. A stone in the north-west corner of the nave still marks its former site. Swift's inscription reads :—

" In hac Area olim habebatur Curia Metropolitica Dublin; et dehinc translata Fuit ad Aedificium

[1] Day and Patton, *Cathedrals of the Church of Ireland*, pp. 123, 129.
[2] Letter to Swift, April 7, 1735.
[3] See Illustration.

positum juxta Parietem Meridionatem Navis, hujus Ecclesia, A.D. 1724 ".

Probably the exterior of the Cathedral was dashed. Contemporary illustrations seem to show bare masonry, but in 1733 we find a receipt for " the sum of 8/9d. for ropes for Mr. Jones ye plasterer to raise the ladders in dashing the church ".[1]

Under the Cathedral flowed the Poddle river—the Ford of the Poddle was the sacred site where St. Patrick had preached. The marshy position caused endless difficulties, and we find Swift constantly dealing with structural damage caused by the damp. An annual fee of £2 10s. was paid to the " Miller of Templeogue " for diverting the waters from overflowing the Cathedral.[2] Outside the building, the stream was bridged over. Occasionally floods prevented the Cathedral from being used for weeks on end ; as we have seen, Bindon's portrait of Swift was transferred for safe keeping to the Deanery on account of the dampness of the Chapter-house.

The inside of the building was plastered and whitened, while the choir was richly painted and gilded. In 1681 a stone roof had been erected there, " painted of an azure colour and inlaid with stars of gold ".[3] An extensive redecoration of the choir took place in 1734.[4]

It has been the habit of nineteenth-century restorers to strip interior stonework ruthlessly, and the modern St. Patrick's has been dealt with in this way. Modern opinion is veering to the old style, still in use in Swift's

[1] Proctor's Accounts, September 26, 1733.
[2] Proctor's Accounts, 1719.
[3] Bernard, *St. Patrick's Cathedral*, p. 16.
[4] Proctor's Accounts, 1734, 5, 6 and 7.

day, of whitening. The Proctor's " Ordinary Accounts " show that one of the regular members of the Cathedral staff was a workman, H. Keating, paid at the rate of nine pounds a year as " plaisterer and whitewasher ". Many entries appear like that of March 19, 1722, when £7 was paid " for whitewashing and painting West window and Gable ".

One of the pleasing witnesses to Swift's care for his church is the constant recurrence of bills for decoration and beautifying, from large works down to tiny items like green velvet cushions for the seats.

A very fair criterion for a churchman's keenness is his enthusiasm for keeping his church decently and in order. In practice it generally works out that a dirty, neglected church means a neglected parish and a careless parson. On this test, Swift's work shows him in a very satisfactory light. The general impression to be had from the accounts is that of a church lovingly cared for. The amount of work done on the fabric is remarkable, even judging by modern standards. For instance, during one year, 1736, the following list of improvements is recorded : painting ; draining and cleaning of the Poddle sewer ; timber covering laid over the Poddle ; smith's work ; five brass clasps for Bibles ; repairing the bells ; mason's and carpenter's work ; carver's work done on the organ ; painting the church doors ; gilding and painting the choir ; glazing ; brasses for the tenor bell ; transcribing the choir books ; a green bag for the chapter books ; taking down and cleaning the candelabra.

Interesting little items from the Cathedral economy of the Swift period are the provision of a new bell, inscribed " Duret illaesa ad preces excitans usque ad sonitum supremae tubae, 1724 " (probably from Swift's pen), the obtaining of a clock with chimes in London by Swift, and the purchase of a fire engine for £20.

Among Swift's more important works for the improvement of the appearance of St. Patrick's was a campaign to erect monuments to notable characters buried in the Cathedral, and to repair existing monuments which were falling into decay.

The Proctor's Accounts show this work in progress— entries are common like that of December 1, 1730— " Seven pounds ten shillings ster. for erecting the Monument by the West door of the Great Isle ".

Swift undertook personally to get this business done, sending out appeals to interested parties. Most of these were successful; but one failed, and the story of its consequence is sufficiently amusing to be re-told in detail.

The Duke of Schonberg, the aged hero of the Battle of the Boyne, had been buried in St. Patrick's, but no monument had ever been erected. Swift wrote to his descendant, Lady Holderness, to have this oversight put right. Unfortunately this lady was unwilling to supply the money necessary and on May 10, 1728, we find Swift writing to Lord Carteret, complaining :—

> " I writ to her myself; and also there was a letter from the dean and chapter, to desire she would order a monument to be raised for him in my Cathedral. It seems Mildmay, now Lord Fitzwalter, her husband, is a covetous fellow; or whatever is the matter, we have had no answer. I desire you will tell Lord Fitzwalter, ' that if he will not send fifty pounds to make a monument for the old duke, I and the chapter will erect a small one of ourselves for ten pounds; wherein it shall be expressed, that the posterity of the Duke, naming particularly Lady Holderness and Mr.

Mildmay, not having the generosity to erect a monument, we have done it of ourselves'. And if, for an excuse, they pretend they will send for his body, let them know it is mine; and rather than send it, I will take up the bones and make it a skeleton and put it in my register office, to be a memorial of their baseness to all posterity. This I expect your excellency will tell Mr. Mildmay, or, as you now call him, Lord Fitzwalter; and I expect likewise, that he will let Sir Conyers D'Arcy know how ill I take his neglect in this matter; although to do him justice, he averred, ' that Mildmay was so avaricious a wretch, that he would let his own father be buried without a coffin, to save charges '."

(By a strange freak of fortune Swift's threat became fact more than a hundred and fifty years later, when the Duke's skull, with a bullet hole through it, was turned up during repairs, and was kept for years in the robing-room as a curio to be shown to visitors !)

Twelve days after this racy outburst Swift wrote again to the Countess of Holderness a polite but rather frigid note, reminding her of her neglect to answer his previous letter and suggesting that " you would please to assign what moderate sum you think fit, to erect a plain marble monument over his Grace ".

After almost exactly two years had passed, and Swift had obtained no satisfaction from the parsimonious Lord Fitzwalter or his Lady, on May 25, 1731, the Chapter agreed to the Schonberg inscription, which is quoted in the Chapter Acts.

" Hic infra situm est corpus Frederici Ducis de
    Schonberg,
  ad Bubindam occisi. A.D. 1690.
  Decanus et Capitulum maximopere etiam atque
    etiam

petierunt, ut haeredes Ducis monumentum in
memoriam paren-
tis erigendum curarent. Sed postquam per
epistolas, per
amicos, diu ac saepe orando nil profecere; hunc
demum
lapidem statuerunt; saltem ut scias hospes ubinam
terrarum
SCHONBERGENSIS cineres delitescunt.
Plus potuit fama virtutis apud alienos quam
sanguinis
proximatas apud suos. A.D. 1731."

It speaks a great deal for the loyalty of the Chapter
to their Dean that this responsible body of reverend
gentlemen should have agreed to Swift's typical but
certainly outrageously startling wording.

With the minimum of delay the black marble tablet
was erected. The Proctor's Accounts give the following
detailed analysis of the cost :—

" Recd. from the Dean and Chapter of St.
Patrick's Dublin the sum of three pounds five
shillings and five pence Ster. towards erecting
Duke Schonberg's Monument. Recd., 4 June
1731, Jonath. Swift."
" Marble table us'd in Duke Schonberg's
Monument—£1. 19. 7."
" The sum of Six pounds sterling for Letter-
cutting, Gold sizing, Guilding &c. Duke Schon-
berg's Monument. Recd. 16 July 1731. Patk.
Laughlin."

Thus the tablet to the memory of Frederick, Duke
Schonberg, was erected at a cost of only 25s. above the
blackmailing minimum of £10 threatened in Swift's
letter to Lord Carteret three years earlier.

There it still stands, after two hundred years, reminding the passer-by how, " in spite of frequent requests by
letter and through friends ", nothing had been done to

commemorate the old Duke, and commenting acidly on the fact that " the memory of his valour was honoured more by strangers in a strange land than by his own flesh and blood ".

Not unnaturally the Dean's action caused considerable offence, even to personages as elevated as the King and Queen of England and the Court of Prussia. " God damn Mr. Swift ", said King George II. " Does he mean to make me quarrel with the King of Prussia ? "

Swift himself professed to have erred upon the side of leniency, writing in the October following to the Countess of Suffolk :—

> " If ever a numerous venerable body of dignified clergymen had reason to complain of the highest repeated indignity, in return of the greatest honour offered by them; to persons they were wholly strangers to, then my chapter is not to be blamed, nor I, who proposed the matter to them; which, however, I would have done by my own authority, but rather chose it should be the work of us all. And I will confess it was upon their advice that I omitted the only two passages which had much bitterness in them; and which a bishop here, one after your own heart, blamed me very much for leaving out; declaring that the treatment given us by the Schonberg family deserved a great deal worse."

Delaney says that Swift originally had desired to insert the words, " Salem ut sciat viator indignabundus, quali in cellula tanti ductoris cineres delitescunt ". By the persuasion of the biographer, he omitted this, " with some other satiric severities ".

Undoubtedly Swift's imperious temper led him astray in this unfortunate episode. But it must be remem-

bered that his original intention was entirely praise-
worthy—to preserve the Cathedral monuments
decently and in order, a policy which he adopted in
all matters connected with St. Patrick's. The Schonberg letter was only one out of a batch written at the
request of the Chapter in May 1729. In a contem-
poraneous letter to the Right Honourable the Lady
Catherine Jones, asking her to repair a family monument, he says, in words which are a model of tact and
style :—

> " Although I am a stranger to your Ladyship's
> person, yet I have heard much of your piety and
> good works, and your Ladyship will easily believe
> that neither the Chapter nor I can have any other
> view in this request than the honour of your family
> (whereof one was Archbishop of Dublin) and the
> care we have of keeping our Cathedral as decently
> as we can ".

This reverent policy of Swift's, which must have
entailed the expenditure of considerable time and
trouble, was remarkably successful, and to his zeal we
owe the preservation of several fine old monuments.

On the north side of the choir is Archbishop Jones's
monument, repaired, together with the family vault
wherein was interred the Earl of Ranelagh, by Lady
Catherine Jones at Swift's request.[1]

On the south wall of the choir (now it is in the nave)
was the huge monument erected early in the reign of
Charles I by Richard, Earl of Cork. For many years
it had been an object of controversy, owing to its
position behind the altar. In 1728 Swift secured its
repair, though not without a certain amount of bickering
with the Earl of Cork and Burlington over an " affront

[1] Mason, *St. Patrick's, Notes and Illustrations*, p. xlix.

he has put upon us, in not answering a letter written to him by the Dean and Chapter ".

Also on the south side of the Nave is the large monument to Narcissus Marsh. The Proctor's Account Books reveal Swift's responsibility for its preservation, for we find in 1728, £10 paid to move Primate Marsh's monument from the churchyard to " the West Isle ".

In the corner of the south transept is a charming little tablet which reveals something of the gentler side of Swift's nature. Archbishop Bernard saw in Swift's portraits the contrast between his fierce eyes with their rugged brows, and the tender, kindly mouth.[1] This friendly little memorial to a faithful servant suggests that the Archbishop was not mistaken in his judgment.

> Here lieth the
> Body of Alex$^{dr.}$
> McGee, servant to
> Dr. Swift, Dean of
> St. Patrick's.
> His gratefull
> Master caused
> this monument
> to be erected in
> memory of his Dis-
> cretion, Fidelity,
> and Diligence
> in that humble
> station
> Ob. Mar. 24 : 1721–2
> Ætat. 29.

It is a pity that some officious friend deterred Swift from putting up the inscription which he originally had in mind—" His Grateful Friend and Master ".[2]

Alexander McGee (known in the Deanery household as " Saunders ") was a real friend. Swift paid a touch-

---

[1] Ball, Introduction by Bernard, p. xliii.
[2] Delaney, *Observations*, p. 132.

ing tribute to him in a letter written to Knightley
Chetwode on March 13, 1722 :—

> " I have the best servant in the world dying in
> the house, which quite disconcerts me. He was
> the first good one I ever had, and I am sure will
> be the last. I know few greater losses in life."

Another cathedral inscription from Swift's pen is
that over the recumbent effigy of Archbishop Tregury,
who died in 1471. It tells how the monument was
found among the ruins of St. Stephen's Chapel, and
re-erected in the nave—probably the item of £7 10s.
in the Proctor's Accounts, mentioned above, relates to
this work. This monument has now been brought
back to its original home.

With the typical precision of Swift, his explanatory
note concludes with the prosaic but useful statement
that for further information about the Archbishop the
student should look up Sir James Ware's book of
reference !

Yet another work of restoration known to be done
by Swift was that on the monuments to Dean Fyshe
—a very fine sixteenth-century brass, which shows the
Dean in kneeling posture. He is a tonsured ecclesiastic
with that peculiar expression of melancholy which was
typical of so many mediaeval brasses. Swift secured
the safety of this memorial; in 1719 it was framed and
replaced on the north side of the altar.[1]

Certainly we owe the Dean a very great debt for his
care of neglected monuments, and for his eagerness to
link up his church with the great history of the past.
In the Chapter Minutes of 1721 we find him appointing
a sub-committee to consider this sort of work, and we

[1] Proctor's Accounts, 1719.

may thank him for that whole policy of preserving old traditions.

The same policy held good with regard to documents. Records were cared for; they were copied; and there was prepared " a room upstairs for a convenient place to keep the records belonging to this Chapter for the better securing and safety of them ".[1] Search was ordered to be made for old papers, and that " an advertisement be printed and published for the finding and discovery of the book commonly called the Dignitas Decani, for which the sum of one pound ten shillings is to be paid by the Proctor to the person that brings the said books ".[1] One is glad to know that the search must have been successful, for the " Dignitas Decani " is now in existence among the Cathedral archives, and is shown in a case in St. Patrick's Baptistry. This action is a pleasing contrast to what happened in quite modern times, when documents bearing Swift's signature were sold promiscuously, and even portions of the Proctor's account books have been cut out as souvenirs. Swift encouraged the preservation of historical records; thus Dr. Lyon was paid by the Chapter for his collection of Cathedral antiquities. It was also by Swift's order that the two handsome engravings of St. Patrick's were made which illustrate Harris's edition of Ware's works. One of these is reproduced in this book.[2]

It is to be noticed that in this picture there is no spire represented. Lovers of architecture may thank Swift for having saved Dublin from a remarkable monstrosity. A few days after Swift had arrived in Dublin he received a letter from Archbishop King, couched in a somewhat dictatorial tone, and informing

[1] Chapter Minutes, 1728.   [2] Page 105.

him that money and designs had been left for the erection of a brick spire on Minot's tower. What a brick spire on top of Gothic masonry would be like may be left to the imagination. Swift contented himself by raising a variety of objections—*e.g.*, that Dublin brick would not stand the smoky atmosphere—and he shelved the whole matter. The existing granite spire was not erected until 1749, or four years after his death.

Before we end this section, two other points of Cathedral administration deserve to be mentioned— Swift's financial genius, and his care for the Cathedral grounds.

Until Swift took over the reins of office the Proctor's annual balance sheet generally showed a loss. Swift was generous in his outlay on repairs to the fabric and for upkeep of the Cathedral, and yet by 1716 he had succeeded in producing a credit balance in the Proctor's books. For almost the first time on record there was a substantial sum in hand at the end of the financial year, and in April 1716 a committee was appointed to invest the surplus of £200.

He adopted a further policy for permanently increasing the Cathedral revenues. It had long been the bad old custom for Deans to accept an immediate cash payment in consideration for the renewal of long leases at the old rents. Accordingly, most of the Cathedral property was let at far less than its proper rent, since the value of Dublin building sites was going up, while the value of money was rapidly decreasing. Swift made it a rule never to accept any fines for renewal when the period of years in a lease came to an end. He always insisted on giving a new lease at an increased rent. According to the custom of the time, this policy meant personal financial loss to Swift himself, but it did ensure that the finances of the Cathedral would be greatly improved in the future.

A typical note in the back of an old lease illustrates Swift's anger at the unscrupulous or foolish methods of under-letting which had formerly been customary :—

> " A lease of Colemine, made by that rascal, Dean Jones, and the knaves or fools, his chapter, to one John Allen, for eighty-one years, to commence from the expiraton of a lease of eighty years, made in 1583; so that there was a lease for one hundred and sixty one years, of two hundred and fifty three acres in Tassagard parish, within three miles of Dublin, for two pounds per annum : this would not expire till the year 1744, and the lands are now, probably worth at the full rent, one hundred and fifty pounds per annum, and so near Dublin could not then be worth less than fifty pounds per annum ".[1]

By renouncing his fines, Swift managed to leave the deanery a much wealthier office when he died than when he first came in to it. Moreover, he improved the value of the estate attaching to the Deanship of Kildare from £120 per annum to £200.

Indeed, Swift's will shows how interested he was in leaving a valuable property for succeeding deans. Thus he expended £600 of his own money on his garden, " Naboth's Vineyard ", and left it by will so that his successor should have it for half that sum.

This humorously named garden brings us to Swift's care for the Cathedral grounds. He was a keen gardener, and happily his taste for trim formality had been developed prior to the fashionable eighteenth-century craze for wild rambling gardens. Especially, Swift loved trees.

[1] January 31, 1714. Quoted in Mason's *St. Patrick's*, p. 174.

In 1721 he set to work to turn the churchyard into a grove. There is a receipt in existence, signed by Swift himself, for £10 8s. from Cathedral funds for making walks and planting trees. It was an attractive if daring idea, for the owners of graves were extremely annoyed. " I disturbed the dead and angered the living ", wrote Swift, " by removing tombstones, that people will be at a loss how to rest with the bones of their ancestors." [1]

However, his elm trees flourished exceedingly, except that a few had to be replaced which were killed by the frosty winter of 1741.

A charming little sketch by J. Franklin shows the finished result half a century later. A top-hatted gentleman and a dainty-waisted lady stroll arm in arm under St. Patrick's rugged grey walls. The green leaves of the elm trees dance beside them in the sun. Among the tombstones blow gay flowers. It is a delightfully fresh pastoral scene, and it might well be a hundred miles away from the bustle of Dublin.[2]

There are still gardens around St. Patrick's Cathedral, and it still is kept as the great Dean would have liked it to be. When night falls we may yet fancy that we see the shade of Jonathan Swift walking with printless steps on the close-cropped grass, enjoying the scent of flowers blown on the evening air.

[1] Letter, December 12, 1721.
[2] Reproduced in Bernard's *St. Patrick's*, p. 65.

CHAPTER VIII

ST. PATRICK'S PULPIT

Swift the Preacher—His Style—Sermon on the Trinity—" On
Sleeping in Church "—The Dozen Surviving Sermons—
His Own Favourite—" On Mutual Subjection "—Hints
for the Mob—" On False Witness "—" On the Poor Man's
Contentment "—Two Sermons against Dissent—" On the
Wretched Condition of Ireland "—Swift and Montaigne—
Sermons at Laracor—Discipline in St. Patrick's—
Criticism for the Novice—The Art of " Handkerchief-
wetting "—Pastor or Preacher?—The Age of Logic—
Simplicity Foremost—Skit on Pedantry—" Letter to a
Young Gentleman "—A Pulpit Prayer.

IT is not easy to estimate the goodness of a preacher
from the mere reading of his sermons years afterwards.
It often happens that the speeches of quite an excellent
orator read badly, while a writer of the brilliance of
Burke could come to be known as the Dinner Bell,
emptying the House of Commons when he rose to
speak.

Accordingly we shall never know just how good or
how bad Swift was as a preacher. We cannot estimate
his personal magnetism—that something which divides
good preachers from bad ones. We may perhaps guess
at it from the fascinating power and charm of some of
his early portraits. But no real information exists
about this. He has left very few sermons behind him,
and scarcely any contemporary criticisms are known
except his own casual remark that he preached political
pamphlets.

However, we do know this—that Swift did take
trouble with his preaching; his theories on how to do

it are unimpeachable, and he had a genuine ambition
to do well.

When he was very young, as he recalled in later
years, he had desired to make a reputation as a preacher.
He would have liked to have heard people inquiring
whether Doctor Swift were preaching that day, and he
would have liked to have seen those folk making special
efforts to get to church in order to listen to him.

All this ambition had to be shelved when he was
thrust into the rough and tumble of party politics—
though indeed his work of presenting ideas forcefully to
the public through the medium of the pamphlet was
no bad training for the effective pulpit work which he
afterwards achieved.

His own sermons possess a plain, direct style infinitely more attractive than the cumbrous periods
fashionable among eighteenth-century divines.   Swift's
ideal of preaching was a simple one—to set forth
concisely what a Christian's duty was, or what a
Churchman ought to believe, and then to prove
convincingly that it must be so.

His Sermon on the Trinity is an example of this
method.   It states the fact of the mystery of the
Trinity, but it does not attempt in any way to explain
it.   Indeed, to Swift's mind, the attempt to explain
the Christian mysteries involved a contradiction, for if
they were explained, then obviously they could remain
mysteries no longer.

This sermon is well worthy of study as a sample
of Swift's straightforward prose style.   Probably no
better-worded statement of this essential doctrine of
Christianity could be made in so brief a space.   In
singularly lucid, simple phraseology, Swift shows of
the Trinity " that there is some kind of unity and dis-

tinction in the divine nature, which mankind can not possibly comprehend; thus the whole doctrine is short and plain, and in itself incapable of any controversy, since God himself both pronounced the fact, but wholly concealed the manner ".

Few theological treatises achieve that crystal-clear simplicity which made Swift's style so satisfying. Dr. Johnson, in his *Lives of the English Poets*, said that Swift's style trickled rather than flowed. Whatever that phrase may have meant, it is quite certain that Dr. Johnson's own ponderous prose never approached Swift's limpid clearness.

His preaching, in the sharp, nervous, unmelodious voice which Delaney describes, set out his arguments crisply and convincingly, and with no attempt at ornament. Swift, after his first youth, never aimed at being admired as a popular preacher. Thus, he wrote to Stella, telling her that he was trying to avoid preaching before the Queen, because every puppy in London would be present, expecting something wonderful, " and be plaguily balked, for I shall preach plain honest stuff ".[1]

Plain, honest stuff he preached, and remarkably effective it must have been. Few men ever knew better how to compose a sermon. His *Letter to a Young Gentleman, Lately Entered into Holy Orders* is one of the most instructive treatises on the art of preaching ever written, and it embodied Swift's own practice. His Trinity Sunday sermon won from John Wesley himself the testimony that " one of the best tracts which that great man, Dean Swift, ever wrote, was his Sermon upon the Trinity ".

Although Swift held himself well in hand and never

[1] *Journal to Stella*, Feb. 14, 1710.

tolerated anything irreverent or humorous in the pulpit, yet sometimes his scorching wit did blaze forth, as when he employed it to dispel effectively the traditional lethargy common among congregations during sermon time. Of this type is his " Sermon on Sleeping in Church ".

In the good-humoured little poem, Baucis and Philemon, when the rustic cottage had magically grown into a church, the double bedstead changed into pews which retained their old tradition of sleepiness. The Dean set out in this sermon to keep the congregation awake in their pews. Indeed, to judge by the careless-ness and indecency of St. Patrick's congregation, reported by Wesley, Swift's method was not un-necessary. Thus, Wesley had to report in his *Journal* under Sunday, July 19, 1752, that he " was greatly shocked by the behaviour of the congregation in St. Patrick's church ", and again, on Sunday, April 23, 1758, he told how he was obliged to join with a neigh-bouring worshipper to reprimand two gentlemen sitting close to him, who " fell a-talking together in the most trifling manner, immediately after they had received the Lord's Supper ".

Taking as his text Acts xx. verse 9, which describes how Eutychus " sunk down with sleep as Paul was long preaching ", Swift began with a couple of ex-hilarating sentences :—

" I have chosen these words with design, if possible, to disturb some part of this audience of some half-an-hour's sleep, for the convenience and exercise whereof this place, at this season of the day, is very much celebrated. Opium is not so stupefying to many persons as an afternoon's sermon." Among sundry causes for the neglect of preaching, he pointed out that none was so destructive as that of sleeping in the House of God. "A scorner may listen to truth and reason, and in time grow serious; an unbeliever may feel the pangs of a guilty conscience; one whose thoughts or eyes wander among other objects may, by a lucky word, be called back to attention. But the sleeper shuts up all avenues to his soul."

We may well imagine how on that Sunday afternoon the careless gallants in St. Patrick's really did refrain from yawning and stretching, and the garrulous beggar-women for once stopped their whispered gossip.

The old high wooden pulpit from which Dean Swift preached is still kept in the north aisle of St. Patrick's Cathedral, together with the Laracor communion table. But only a mere handful out of all his sermons survive to-day. He never troubled to preserve them for publication—indeed, we hear of his having casually given away a collection of thirty-five of them to Sheridan, saying, "There are a bundle of my old sermons. You may have them if you please; they may be of use to you, they never were of any to me." For all that, each one of the dozen which remain is interesting and worthy of study. Their titles are as follows :—

1. The Difficulty of Knowing One's Self.
2. On the Trinity.
3. On Mutual Subjection.
4. On the Testimony of Conscience.
5. On Brotherly Love.
6. On the Martyrdom of King Charles I.
7. On False Witness.
8. On the Poor Man's Contentment.
9. On the Causes of the Wretched Condition of Ireland.

10. On Sleeping in Church.
11. On the Wisdom of this World.
12. On Doing Good.

The last mentioned of these was Swift's favourite sermon. It consists of an appeal for patriotism, meaning thereby public-spiritedness. It explains how it is necessary for even the humblest citizen to act for the public good. All wilful injuries done to the public rank as very great sins in the sight of God. The example which Swift quoted was the project for coining Wood's Halfpence—that disgraceful piece of jobbery which was quashed so effectively by the Drapier.

" I never preached but twice in my life, and they were not sermons but pamphlets ", said Swift. On being asked on what subject they were, he answered, " They were against Wood's Halfpence ".[1] Of this sermon, Burke said that it contained perhaps the best motives to patriotism ever contained within so small a compass.[2]

To the modern reader perhaps the finest of Swift's sermons—apart from his doctrinal exposition of the Trinity—is that upon Mutual Subjection. It is the least topical of all, and consequently it has dated least. And of all, it is the most remarkable for neatness of construction.

Mutual Subjection is that duty which each member of the family of mankind owes to each other member. It is something more tangible than " the compliments, of course, when our betters are pleased to tell us they are our humble servants, but understand us to be their slaves ". It means, in essence, doing our daily work

[1] Mrs. Pilkington's Memoirs.
[2] Quoted by Lecky, *Leaders of Public Opinion in Ireland, Swift*, p. 21.

in the spirit that such work will be for the benefit of
the whole community, and not for mere selfish gain.
Those who fall short of this standard are " perfect
nuisances in a commonwealth, as are usually princes
who are born with no more advantages of strength or
wisdom than other men ; and by an unhappy education
are usually more defective in both than thousands of
their subjects ". The truth is, that it is impossible
for one member of a State to subsist without the active
co-operation of his fellows. In other words, Mutual
Subjection means Mutual Dependence, and it carries
with it a duty to our neighbours, to do to them as we
would that they should do to us.

If this duty were to be genuinely practised by men,
at least four valuable results would follow :—

First of all, the vice of pride would be extinguished,
for we should then realize that, whatever our own
talents might be, other men also possessed talents of a
different kind which were being used for our own
benefit.

The possession of riches would at last be seen in its
proper light—as a stewardship. Wealth, as Swift
pointed out, is not property, but a trust. (He himself,
it is said, laid out an exact third of his income on
charity.)

Thirdly, the happiness of mankind would be increased
by the rooting out of envy and malice—for obviously
we could not be envious of a man if we realized that we
depended upon his co-operation for the supplying of
our own wants.

Lastly, we should learn to be content with our
respective stations in life, knowing that other men
with greater advantages were using those advantages
for our own benefit.

The conclusion is this :—

> " God has sent us into the world to obey His commands, by doing as much good as our abilities will reach, and as little evil as our many infirmities will permit.   Some He has only trusted with one talent, some with five, and some with ten.   No man is without his talent; and he that is faithful or negligent in a little, shall be rewarded or punished, as well as he that hath been so in a great deal."

A very delightful feature of Swift's sermons was the way in which he could give homely practical advice to simple people.   He knew intimately, and he loved well, his humble congregation from the Liberties, and he spoke to them in terms which even the illiterate could understand.   Thus, his sermon, " On False Witness ", concludes with a set of elementary rules for avoiding getting into trouble at the mouths of informers. Have nothing to do with politics, said Swift.   Do not be afraid of displaying your loyalty to the King—as well as being advantageous to yourself, it is a good Christian practice, for the powers that be are ordained by God.   Avoid intemperance, for that will lead you into saying dangerous things.   " If it be often so hard for men to govern their tongues when they are in their right senses, how can they hope to do it when they are heated with drink ? "   Above all, refrain carefully from the folly of arguing about politics in public places.

In much the same vein was his sermon " On the Poor Man's Contentment ".   It, too, was obviously addressed to the humbler majority of St. Patrick's congregation—the weavers and workmen and pensioners of Swift's Little Kingdom, " the honest, industrious, artificer, the meaner sort of tradesmen and the

labouring man," the cripples, the one legged pathetic
" Stumpa-Nymphas " whom he supported,[1] the para-
lysed " poor Hussey " [2] who got " one British shilling
a week " out of the Cathedral economy.

After a preliminary word of encouragement that they
should persevere in honest industry, Swift pointed out
the benefits which the poor possess—health, sound
sleep, freedom from hatred and the goading of ambition.
On the other hand, the rich live under many
disadvantages.

> " Business, fear, guilt, design, anguish and
> vexation are continually buzzing about the curtains
> of the rich and the powerful, and will hardly suffer
> them to close their eyes, unless when they are
> dosed with the fumes of strong liquors."

Indeed, remarked the Dean, he knew of no advantage
which the rich had over the poor, unless it be that of
doing good to others; " but this is an advantage which
God hath not given wicked men the grace to make
use of ".

His sermon on the Martyrdom of King Charles I is
interesting as another example and statement of Swift's
dislike for dissent. He describes here the gradual
efforts of " these wicked Puritans " to break up the
Established Church, beginning in Queen Elizabeth's
time to quarrel with small externals such as surplices,
ecclesiastical vestments, the ring in matrimony, and
the sign of the Cross in baptism, and gradually increasing in violence to a pitch which " must needs have the
whole government of the Church dissolved ".

He would scarcely admit the right of the dissenters
to be described as Christians.

[1] Delaney's *Observations*, p. 92.
[2] Proctor's Accounts, 1736.

"Neither will the bare name of Protestants set them right, for surely Christ requires more from us than a bare profession of hating Popery, which a Turk or an Atheist may do as well as a Protestant."

Another sermon in a not dissimilar vein, is that on "Brotherly Love"—a title which scarcely prepares the reader for the savage attack which he made on the Roman Catholics and the Dissenters !

"This nation of ours hath for a hundred years past been infested by two enemies, the Papists and Fanatics; who, each in their turns, filled it with blood and slaughter, and, for a time destroyed both the Church and government", said Swift in the opening paragraph. He then went on to describe their "inroads and insolence", which he took to be the principal causes of the hatred and animosity which reigned in Ireland at that time.   The conclusion he arrived at was this :—

"In order to restore brotherly love, let me earnestly exhort you to stand firm in your religion. I mean, the true religion hitherto established among us, without varying in the least either to Popery on one side or to Fanaticism on the other; and in a particular manner beware of that word, moderation, and believe it, that your neighbour is not immediately a villain, a Papist and a traitor, because the fanatics and their adherents will not allow him to be a moderate man."

Least of all like the conventional sermon is that on the "Causes of the Wretched Condition of Ireland". This is practically a summary of his various published opinions about the country, and it is a political rather than a religious work.   Its vigorous phrasing expresses finely Swift's outraged sense of justice and his burning indignation at the systematic way in which the Ireland of his day was maladministered with cold-blooded calculation.

His bitter enemy, Bishop Evans of Meath, once likened an Ash-Wednesday Sermon of Swift's to one of Montaigne's essays.

The criticism is not without a certain amount of insight. In style the two writers were rather similar. They differed in constructive power; Swift's sermons were logically and neatly planned; Montaigne wrote rather as the flow of association of ideas led him. But in language both worked on the same lines; both employed a simple, vigorous, colloquial style which is easy and compelling. Montaigne's estimate of his own style might well have been applied to Swift's prose.

> " Le parler que j'aime, c'est un parler simple et naïf, et tel sur le papier qu' à la bouche, un parler succulent et nerveux, court et serré . . . éloigné d'affectation, déréglé, décousu et hardi. . . . Puisse—je ne me servir que des mots qui servent aux halles à Paris." [1]

No doubt Evans' criticism was meant to be derogatory, and as such it probably bore the more obvious innuendo that Swift was a sceptic like Montaigne. If this thought were in the Bishop's mind, he was very wide of the mark. Swift was no sceptic. However his natural genius under other circumstances might have turned him towards that direction, we have seen that his ecclesiastical training and environment had made him a sincere churchman and a convinced believer in the truths of revealed religion. Lecky sums up this side of Swift's character very accurately.

> " It may seem strange that an intellect at once so powerful and so irreverent as that of Swift

[1] Montaigne, Vol. I, p. 25.

should have been wedded to High Church notions, but the fact is undoubted, and it is an entire mis-representation to describe these sentiments as lightly or hastily assumed. . . . He said on one occasion that he could not understand a clergyman not being a High Churchman. . . . That he would have been a sceptic if he had not been a High Churchman is very probable, but this is no disparagement to his sincerity." [1]

Although Swift never regarded himself as a great preacher, he did his duty conscientiously in the pulpit. In the cathedral he was regular in his turn, and in his Laracor days he preached alternate Sundays with his curate to his congregation of fifteen, " mostly gentle and all simple ".

In the wider sphere of St. Patrick's he was equally diligent in enforcing the regular duty of preaching, and in improving the prevailing standard. A trenchant marginal note in the Chapter Minutes of 1724 orders that a letter should be sent to Dean Burnett to intimate that if he did not pay the sum of twenty shillings " due from him to the clergyman that preached his turn in the Choir of St. Patrick's, a Sequestration will issue against him "—the Dean would tolerate nothing slipshod in the Cathedral routine !

Nor had he any toleration for negligent and incompetent pulpit oratory. At Windsor he remarked that the Queen's absence from church was " all for the better, for we had a dunce to preach ", and on another occasion he spoke scathingly of a " sad, pert, dull parson who preached at Kensington ".[2]

Happily he did not confine himself to destructive

[1] Lecky, *Leaders of Public Opinion in Ireland, Swift*, pp. 12 and 21.
[2] *Journal to Stella*, September 30 and July 15, 1711.

criticism—as most critics of bad preachers do. He set to work carefully to raise the standard of St. Patrick's preaching, especially among the younger men. His methods were salutary, though they must have been disconcerting to a nervous performer. Delaney tells how he pulled out paper and pencil when anyone got into the pulpit, " and carefully noted every wrong pronounciation or expression that fell from him. Whether too hard, or scholastic (and of consequence not sufficiently intelligible to a vulgar hearer) or such as he deemed in any degree improper, indecent, slovenly or mean ; and those, he never failed to admonish the preacher of as soon as he came into the Chapter House." [1]

Simplicity, clearness, and logical reasoning were the essentials which Swift practised, and which he expected in other people's sermons. He had no patience with the emotional type of preaching which was characteristic of the " Fanatics "—Dissenters and Independents—and he had a supreme scorn for the art of what he called " Handkerchief Wetting ".

> " A plain convincing Reason may possibly operate upon the Mind both of a learned and ignorant Hearer as long as they live, and will edify a thousand Times more than the Art of wetting the Handkerchiefs of a whole congregation, if you were sure to attain it ".[2]

Some of his most boisterous satire was levelled against those gusty orators, whose pulpit stock-in-trade lay in the rousing of the emotions of simple people.

" It is to be understood ", he wrote in the *Essay on*

---

[1] Delaney's *Observations*, p. 140.
[2] *Letter to a Young Gentleman.*

the Mechanical Operation of the Spirit, " that, in the language of the spirit, cant and droning supply the place of sense and reason in the language of men : because, in spiritual harangues, the disposition of the words according to the art of grammar has not the least use." In that outspoken work of his youth, *The Tale of a Tub,* he identified with very frank ribaldry, wind and spirit, holding the former to be the motive power of all preachers who claimed to give utterance as the spirit moved them.

Emotional religion and emotional preaching received little sympathy from Swift. Apparently he had no real belief in the power of preaching to make conversions, and most of his sermons are as unlike typical mission preaching as can be imagined. As he himself said, " The Preaching of Divines helps to preserve well-inclined Men in the Course of Virtue, but seldom or never reclaims the Vicious ".[1] Delaney's pen-picture of the Dean's house-to-house visitations in Dublin suggests that Swift looked for spiritual results from pastoral work rather than from the pulpit. There can be no doubt that Swift was a very fine parish clergyman and his sermons were those of a pastor of a congregation rather than of a revivalist.

Admittedly his preaching was tinged overmuch with the religious coldness of the eighteenth century. Sir Walter Scott, who belonged to a later generation which had been nourished upon the romantic revival and which was familiar with the warmer appeal of the Wesleyan teaching, criticized Swift for his lack of fire. His sermons, Scott said, " had none of that thunder which appals, or that resistless and winning softness which melts the hearts of an audience. He can never

[1] *Thoughts on Various Subjects.*

have enjoyed the triumph of uniting hundreds in one ardent sentiment of love, of terror, or of emotion." [1]

That is scarcely a fair criticism. Swift lived in an age of logic, and he belonged to an educated society which had revolted against the excesses of fanatical dissenters. During the period in which Swift occupied the pulpit, the evangelistic kind of sermon was practically unheard of from the clergy, or at any rate from those of the Established Church. For that period his sermons do display a good deal more of genuine Christian feeling than was common at the time. The pendulum had swung in the British Isles to a frigid intellectualism in Church matters. It was possible for Blackstone to say that in no London church was there any Christian teaching to be heard more definite in tone than that which might have been derived from the works of Cicero. Only a few clergy—among whom was Swift—preserved anything of the warmth of the old High-Church tradition. Its best exponents—the Non-juring bishops and clergy—had ceased with their expulsion from the Church to be an active voice. The Evangelical revival was yet to come. Wesley's first open-air preaching did not begin until 1739, when Swift's work was all but over. And during all his career, Swift had learned to distrust—unduly, perhaps —religious appeal to the feelings and sentiments of his public. He professed never to have known any abiding benefit from such an appeal; the results of impassioned eloquence calculated to play upon the feelings lasted, he once said, not longer than dinner-time on the same Sunday.

Quite a casual glance at Swift's own sermons impresses the reader with their simplicity and their ease.

[1] Scott's Ed. of Swift, 1824; note on Vol. VII, p. 403.

He avoided erudite and technical words, modelling his preaching so that it could be understood by the dullest intelligence in his congregation. He was under no illusions as to what that level of intelligence was, adopting Lord Falkland's standard, that when he doubted whether a word were perfectly intelligible or no, he used to consult one of his Lady's Chambermaids ![1]

One of Swift's more amusing skits is a model of a letter sent by the village schoolmaster to a young country clergyman who was addicted to long words. It purports to be written " in a style as near as he could to your own ", in order that it might be acceptable to the preacher. It pleads, with delightful burlesque, for a somewhat more comprehensible pulpit style which would be suited to a country congregation :—

> " We do, from the nadir of our rusticity, alma-cantarize to the very zenith of your unparalleled sphere of activity, in beseeching your exuberant genius to nutriate our rational appetites with intelligible theology, suited to our plebean apprehensions, and to recondite your acroamaticall locutions for more scholastic auscultators."

This typical squib of Swift's states part of that theory of preaching which he set out more fully in his *Letter to a Young Gentleman Lately Entered into Holy Orders*.

This pamphlet is perhaps the very finest of Swift's serious works. It is still extraordinarily up to date; when we compare the theory of preaching which it advocates with the customary florid standard of the eighteenth century, it is obvious that Swift was two centuries ahead of his time. It is a pity that the *Letter to a Young Gentleman* is not better known—even

[1] *Letter to a Young Gentleman.*

to-day it would be valuable as a text-book in theological colleges.

In order to analyse Swift's methods, a close study of this book is essential, and it proves extraordinarily interesting.

The letter opens with a word of regret that the young gentleman had not spent some further time at study in the University before he had entered into Holy Orders. The average run of young men were ordained far too early, and very rarely did they manage to rise above a country curacy—unless they were lucky enough to be friendly with some bishop " who happens to be not overstocked with Relations or attach'd to Favourites, or is content to supply his Diocese without Colonies from England ", and who might possibly bestow upon them some unimportant living.

Under such circumstances, Swift is regretfully forced to admit that a properly educated and well-read body of clergy was almost impossible.

The Dean then goes on to give detailed instruction on how to learn to preach. The first essential is practice—there can be no substitute for that. Preferably the tyro should try himself out upon a scattered country congregation—because in that case there will be fewer to suffer ! It is necessary during this period to have a competent critic in the congregation to give hints about faults and affectations, for these are things which otherwise may become life-long habits.

A good English style should be cultivated. " Proper Words in proper places, makes the true Definition of a Style." Without going into the whole matter in detail, Swift points out some of the commonest faults in style.

The first is the use of obscure terms " which by the

K

Women are called hard Words, and by the better sort
of Vulgar, fine Language ". Young clergymen are
especially addicted to the vice of using professional
jargon. At all costs, simplicity must be maintained,
so that even the most unlearned may understand
without straining his intelligence.

Above all, the use of technical theological terms
should be avoided. Many clergy seem to think that
it is the duty of the congregation to understand these
words—" which I am sure it is not ". Of this type
are words like "Omniscience, Ubiquity, Beatific Vision ",
etc., and also some of the difficult terms of Scripture,
which ought to be translated into simple King's English.

The opposite to pedantry is equally undesirable—that
is to say, an affectation of the racy style of the taverns
and the coffee-houses; the Slovenly and the Indecent.

To sum up about style :—

> " When a Man's thoughts are clear, the properest
> Words will generally offer themselves first, and his
> own Judgment will direct him in what order to
> place them, so they may be best understood.
> Where Men err against this Method, it is usually
> on purpose, and to show their Learning, their
> Oratory, their Politeness, or their Knowledge of
> the World. In short, that Simplicity, without
> which no human Performance can arrive to any
> great Perfection, is nowhere more eminently useful
> than in this [the pulpit]."

Swift does not recommend his pupil to attempt to
arouse the emotions of his congregation. As we have
seen, it was not his own practice to do so. He looked
on Demosthenes as a superior orator to Cicero, because
the former appealed to the reason and understanding
of his hearers, the latter to their affections. " I do not

see ", he says, " how this talent of moving the Passions can be of any great use towards directing Christian Men in the Conduct of their Lives, at least in these Northern Climates." If the arguments of a preacher are strong, he should set them out in as powerful a manner as possible, reasonably and sensibly. But he should beware of allowing the pathetic part of his discourse to swallow up the rational, for passion should never prevail over reason.

The real purpose of a sermon is to set out and to prove convincingly the elements of Christian ethics and dogma. As this can only be done by simple explanation and argument, the heads of sections and the steps of reasoning should be firmly and concisely stated. Otherwise the discourse will become hard to follow, and the entire value will be lost.

Some useful practical hints on delivery follow. Swift prefers sermons to be spoken without notes, but if that is impossible to the preacher, a sermon may be read in such a way as to appear extempore. The way to do this is to be careful in the preparation of the manuscript. It should be written in a large, clear hand on generously sized sheets of paper, without corrections, and with paragraphs, headings, and expression marks clearly shown. In that way the preacher may " cheat his people by making them believe he had it all by heart ". Read sermons often fail just because they have been scribbled carelessly; bad writing often makes the preacher hold his head down within an inch of the cushion, to read what is hardly legible ; other preachers for the same reason develop a trick of popping up and down every moment, from their paper to the congregation, " like an idle Schoolboy on a Repetition Day ".

Next comes a wise warning against the cheap and easy habit of decrying the heathen philosophers. Actually, as Swift points out, they were monotheists, and the exponents of a very high code of morality. They failed to grip the world, not so much because they were wrong in what they taught, but because their teaching lacked that sort of divine sanction which Christianity possesses. Accordingly they ought to be read and studied diligently, and most certainly they should not be abused ignorantly by men who know nothing about them.

Quotations should be employed very sparingly, except those from Scripture and from the Fathers. Moreover, they should be used fairly and in their proper context—casual tags of Scripture twisted out of their real sense are meaningless. " Some of you conceive you have no more to do than to turn over a Concordance, and there having found the principal Word, introduce as much of the Verse as will serve your Turn, though in reality it makes nothing for you." Despite Swift's warnings more than two centuries ago, the habit of proving theological arguments by the use of irrelevant texts still obtains to a regrettable degree !

For the reason that he liked simplicity, Swift disliked intensely the display of Greek and Latin in the pulpit. It was a wonder, he thought, that the Dissenters did not object to the use of the latter as a relic of Popery !

Commonplace books he distrusted too. Generally he found them to be nothing more than sterile collections of platitudes. The better method for providing sound material for sermons was by judicious and regular reading. Swift agreed with Bacon that reading made a full man, and that it gradually and imperceptibly provided a good turn to a man's thoughts and reasoning without overloading his memory or without even making him conscious of any change for the better. (We may notice here that Swift's own style exemplifies this. Its richness and intelligence were obviously the fruit of deep reading, but that reading was so digested and assimilated that it became Swift's own. No style shows less direct borrowing from other authors than does Swift's.)

It is to be noted, he said, that that same well-developed mind which is the result of sound reading does not call for any display of obscure erudition. It expresses itself rather in simple, well-balanced phrasing. And so Swift has a few scathing words for those scholars who appear to find it desirable to fill their sermons with " Philosophical Terms and Notions of the metaphysical or abstracted Kind, which generally have one Advantage, to be equally understood by the Wise, the Vulgar, and the Preacher himself. I have been better entertained, and more informed by a Chapter in the Pilgrim's Progress, than by a long Discourse upon the Will and the Intellect, and Simple or Complex Ideas."

Indeed, metaphysics have little place at all in the preacher's work. Swift himself, as we remember from stories of his college days, never could settle down to the abstractions of the philosophers, and he believed that the Christian mysteries ought to remain as mysteries. On the great festivals it is the preacher's duty to set out the teaching of the Church—but he does not find that any clergyman " is directed in the Canons or Articles, to attempt explaining the Mysteries of the Christian Religion. And indeed, since Providence intended there should be mysteries, I do not see how it can be agreeable to Piety, Orthodoxy, or good Sense, to go about such a Work."

The letter continues with a lengthy estimate of the
free-thinkers—people who, to Swift's mind, are generally not thinkers at all, but mostly ignorant and
vicious boors, drunkards, and the scum of society. As
these folk are generally not in church, it is inadvisable
to spend too much time scolding the righteous for the
faults of those who are not present to hear.

Lastly, Swift expresses the hope that the Clergy
" have almost given over perplexing themselves and their
Hearers, with abstruse Points of Predestination, Election,
and the like, at least, it is time they should ; and therefore I shall not trouble you further upon this Head ".

So concludes this remarkably acute text-book of
preaching.

Enough has been said to show that Swift was at least
a sincere preacher, and that he took remarkable pains
to be a good one.   On the question of his whole religious
outlook, this fact is informative. If Swift were a
sceptic, as has been alleged, surely no other sceptic
ever gave himself such trouble to teach the Christian
message or to reduce its presentation to such a fine
art.   That admirable *Letter to a Young Gentleman* was
written only a few years after the Earl of Nottingham,
speaking in the debate on the Schism Act, had described
Swift as " a divine who is hardly suspected of being a
Christian ".   The tone of the *Letter*, the feeling which
runs through it all, is proof of the falseness of the
charge.   It makes certain Swift's very sincere allegiance
to his Church, and his Christianity.

Suggestive of that evangelical feeling which, too
often, Swift kept hidden within his heart, is his
customary pulpit prayer :—

"Almighty and most merciful God ! forgive us
all our sins. Give us grace heartily to repent

them, and to lead new lives. Graft in our hearts
a true love and veneration for thy holy name and
word. Make thy pastors burning and shining
lights, able to convince gainsayers, and to save
others and themselves. Bless this congregation
here met together in thy name : grant them to
hear and receive thy holy word, to the salvation
of their own souls. Lastly we desire to return
thee praise and thanksgiving for all thy mercies
bestowed upon us; but chiefly for the Fountain
of them all. Jesus Christ our Lord, in whose
name and words we further call upon thee saying,
' Our Father '."

CHAPTER IX

ST. PATRICK'S CHOIR

ANOTHER interesting chapter in Swift's deanship was his handling of the choir. When he came to office the choir was very far from what it should have been. At once Swift set about improving discipline and quality.

The Dean was most energetic in ensuring that the members of the choir should be the very best performers that could be had, and no influence could obtain a position for a singing-man if he were not competent. That was an inflexible rule of Swift's. Thus, when Lady Carteret applied to him to obtain a vicarage for a nominee of her own, his reply was a refusal—in characteristic vein. If only she had desired his assistance to obtain a deanery or a bishopric for one of her friends, he professed that he would have been glad to help, since efficiency was not essential in those latter offices. However, he regretted that he must refuse her present request, on the grounds that the competency of a vicar choral was put to the test daily.

He scoured the British Isles for suitable material. Candidates for the choir were brought from England

SWIFT'S BUST AND EPITAPH IN ST. PATRICK'S CATHEDRAL.

[Facing p. 143

to have their voices tested. We read in the Proctor's Accounts of September 1719 that one such was paid four moyders to go back to England, " not being liked ". Three years later two other candidates were sent over for trial from Windsor by the Reverend Andrew Knape. One of these, Mr. Elford, was recommended to Swift as " a good choirman ". Unfortunately, he too failed to come up to Swift's standard. Of the second Knape wrote, " He was a very useful chorister to us. His voice since its breaking is somewhat harsh, but I believe will grow mellower." [1] We do not know whether this singer was more successful, as his name was not given in Knape's letter.

Swift's search for choristers was indefatigable. In a letter from London to the Dean's Vicar, he wrote, " I got no voice in Oxford, but am endeavouring for one here ".[2] He pressed his English friends into the search. A lengthy correspondence with Arbuthnot exists on the subject of potential vicars. Arbuthnot was by way of being a minor composer—he was responsible for an anthem, " As pants the hart "—hence he had to bear the brunt of Swift's musical negotiations. On September 20, 1726, he wrote to the Dean :—

> " Your negotiation with the singing-man is in the hands of my daughter Nancy, who, I can assure you, will neglect nothing that concerns you ; she has wrote about it ".

Swift kept on writing to Arbuthnot and pressing him for this singer, for on November 8 Arbuthnot replied in a rather nervously apologetic sort of tone :—

> " It is not Nanny's fault, who has spoke several times to Dr. Pepusch about it, and writ three or

[1] Letter to Swift, April 23, 1722.
[2] Letter, April 16, 1726.

four letters and received for an answer that he would write for the young fellow; but still nothing is done."

Eventually the elusive chorister was secured, one William Fox, who was a member of Swift's Choir from 1727 until his death in 1734. Swift notes that he paid off Fox's debts to Arbuthnot " like an honest man ", five guineas lent. This same Fox was later to prove a trial to Swift, as we shall have occasion to notice.

Arbuthnot was kept busy in search of material for St. Patrick's. On May 8, 1729, he wrote :—

" I recommend one Mr. Mason, son of Mason, gentleman of the Queen's chapel, a baritone voice, for the vacancy of a singer in your Cathedral. . . . I believe you will hardly get better. He has a pleasant baritone voice and has sung several times in the King's Chapel this winter, to the satisfaction of the audience. I answer for this."

John Mason was one of Swift's successes. He had a long career as a singer and composer, was Christ's Church Vicar from 1732 until his death in 1784, and was Archdeacon of Dublin's Vicar from 1759.

Hardly had Arbuthnot secured Mason, when he was at work again. On June 9 we find him writing, " I have been inquiring about a counter-tenor, but have as yet, no intelligence of any ".

This sort of correspondence goes on for years, testifying to Swift's anxiety and interest for St. Patrick's music.

When Swift arrived at Dublin he found the discipline of the choir very lax. The eighteenth century was a notoriously careless age in Church matters, and St. Patrick's was in every way slipshod until Swift took

over the reins of office. Immediately discipline was
stiffened. As early as 1714 it was ordered that " all
the Vicars Choralls in this Church do attend the
Cathedral service of this Church every Sunday and
Holy Day in the Morning, and that this act or order do
commence on Sunday the eleventh of this instant ".[1]
Dr. Johnson says that Swift attended the evening
anthem to see that it was not negligently performed [2]—
also, no doubt, to keep a check on attendance, for
choirmen did their best to escape from Sunday evening
church.

Occasionally Swift had to take special disciplinary
action. There is preserved an entertaining summary
of the faults of Mr. Fox and Mr. Church, two of the
vicars. One fault of the former was that he rarely
sang at all, pleading constant colds : this happened
so very often, commented Swift, that it must be entirely
his own fault, and that therefore he deserved " a
severe animadversion ". Moreover, Fox appeared in
church " dirty, filthy, and very indecent ", and sometimes even intoxicated. " Let this time be a caution
to you ", wrote Swift. " If you do not amend this
you shall receive an admonition."

If Mr. Fox was a disreputable and unwashed ruffian,
Mr. Church must have been even more annoying to an
officiating minister. His indictment runs as follows :—

> " Very indecent in his behaviour, openly laugh-
> ing, grinning, whispering in the time of Divine
> Service ; he and Mr. Fox disputing constantly
> the performance of an anthem ; and will not agree
> upon it, perhaps, or come to a resolution till almost
> the instant of performing it. So remedy this.
> My Vicar or the Chantors shall in due time before

[1] Chapter Minutes.
[2] Johnson, *Lives of the English Poets, Swift.*

prayers name the Anthem, or if any particular Anthem be required by any Dignitary in his attendance, I expect it shall be performed, under a severe penalty." [1]

One of Swift's few lapses from respectability in the Church precincts is connected with another recalcitrant choirman who had grievously offended the Dean. He had absented himself from Church, until he suddenly reappeared one Sunday morning and began the anthem, which happened to be " Whither shall I go, whither shall I go, whither shall I fly, from Thy Presence? "

" To jail, you dog, to jail! " growled the Dean in an audible voice. But we are told that there was a happy ending, for " the next morning he forgave the poor sinner on his promise of amendment ".[2]

The body of Vicars Choral were firmly handled, too, when they attempted to make leases without due consent from the Dean and Chapter. A renewal of the Earl of Abercorn's valuable holding in York Street was given in this way in 1713, and immediately trouble started. The Dean hastened into the fray, determined to preserve the privileges of the Chapter. In December 1713 he wrote from London to the Reverend John Worrall (Dean's Vicar and head of the Vicars Choral, and afterwards one of Swift's closest and most reliable friends) :—

> " I received last post your letter relating to a lease to be made to my Lord Abercorn by the Vicars Choral. I desire you will let the vicars know that I shall to the utmost resent their presuming to make any lease without the consent of the Dean and Chapter, which they are bound to have by their own subscriptions.

[1] Visitation of 1734 (MSS. in St. Patrick's Cathedral).
[2] B. Newman, *Jonathan Swift*, p. 220.

"Let them know further that I am very well instructed in my own power both from the late Dean and from Dr. Synge, and that I will immediately deprive every man of them who consents to any lease without the approbation aforesaid, and shall think the Church well rid of such men, who to gratify their unreasonable avarice would starve their successors. I shall write this post to Dr. Synge to take the proper measures on this occasion. I desire you will read this letter to the Vicars, and let them count upon it that I will be as good as my word."

This letter (as we may imagine), did nothing to placate the Vicars, who had not yet learnt that Swift must be obeyed. The dispute dragged on indefinitely. In June 1714 Swift mentioned in a letter to Archdeacon Walls that he was determined to call the Vicars to account to the utmost that he was able. Three months later the matter was in the hands of the lawyers, who informed the Dean and Chapter that their case was a good one. "My desires in that point are very moderate", said Swift, "only to break the lease and turn out nine singing men".[1] At the end of March 1715 it appeared that the case was coming to an issue, for the trial prevented Swift from going to Trim as he had planned.[2] But even by the end of June the case was not finally settled. On the 28th of the month Swift wrote the Pope that "my amusements are defending my small dominions against the Archbishop, and endeavouring to reduce my rebellious choir".

During November of the same year the Chapter Minutes record that the Vicars Choral were ordered to

[1] Letter, September 27, 1714.
[2] Letter, March 31, 1715.

give their final answer. Eventually we find them chastened and back again at their posts, but not without having suffered for their rashness in defying the Dean. By way of punishment in 1717 it was ordered, " that the money forfeited by the Vicars Chorals for their absence and neglect of their duty in the Cathedral be disposed of in wainscotting the Vicar's Hall ".[1]

From that time forward the sanction of the Dean and Chapter for making leases was sought as a matter of course by the one-time rebellious choir. Thus, in April 1721 it was ordered by the Chapter " that the Vicars Chorals have leave to make a lease in Thomas Street ".[1]

Perhaps, though, their conduct did not always continue perfect, for a little later we find an account for £1 10s. for " a new Coppy in Parchment of the Vicars' Statutes " ! [1]

Having seen how Swift subdued his choir, we may now study the way in which he organized the Cathedral music. For this the Proctor's Accounts and the Chapter Minutes are full of interesting items of information.

Swift's choir expenditure was generous. A fine organ had been placed in the Cathedral in 1695 at the great cost of £855, plus the old one, as we should say nowadays, in part exchange. Over it were placed the Ormond arms, which Swift valiantly preserved after the Duke's attainder. This organ existed—rebuilt many times—up to the beginning of the twentieth century.

Mrs. Pilkington—writing in her *Memoirs* with that proper awe for Swift and all his works which she always displayed—remarked specially on the beauty of the

[1] Chapter Minutes.

" fine organ ", which with " its antique magnificence and so harmonious a choir " recalled to her poetical mind some of Milton's more sonorous lines.

Swift cared for this instrument as it deserved to be cared. Among the Cathedral servants he retained at a cost of £10 per annum a permanent organ-tuner, one Philip Hollister. In later years this person went up in the world, and became the proprietor of the fashionable Ranelagh Pleasure Gardens. In 1730 additions were made, £50 being spent on " the Bassoon and Sexquialter Stops, added to the Cathedral Organ ". A little later a case and locks were provided, to keep unauthorized people from tampering with the new stops. And we find frequent mentions of " sailcloth " being purchased to cover the organ during the periodic white-washings of the interior.

The organists during Swift's career were two, Daniel and Ralph Roseingrave, father and son, and members of a talented if occasionally erratic musical family. Daniel had been successively organist of Winchester, Salisbury, and Christ Church, Dublin, before he was appointed to St. Patrick's. In March 1719 he resigned in favour of his son, and until two years after Swift's death Ralph was retained as organist at £30 a year.

Here and there through the Proctor's Accounts we find his name—thus in 1736 we find the Chapter allowing him £2 10s. over and above his salary for composing and setting thirty anthems (surely not excessive pay !).

Indeed, to judge by the number of new anthems composed and paid for throughout Swift's deanship, and by the rapid revisions and renewals of service books, the choir seems to have been kept busy.

A few examples at random may be given from the receipt books.

> " To John Mason for Twenty-five new anthems, seventeen pounds."
> " Received from ye Rev. Dean and Chapter &c. ye sum of twenty and six pounds Ster. on acct. of writing and pricking new musick books for ye use of ye choir."
> " Received the sum of Nine Pounds and Two Shillings; being their first subscription towards Doctor Greene's Forty Select Anthems in score for use of the Cathedral."

Although Swift claimed to be no musician, it is quite obvious that he worked unremittingly to improve the standard of singing in the Cathedral. In one of his rare letters touching on Church matters, he wrote to Harley of his choir in a typically flippant manner which scarcely concealed his genuine interest.

> " I have the honour to be captain of a band of musicians including boys . . . and I understand music like a Muscovite; but my choir is so degenerate under the reigns of former Deans of famous memory, that the race of people called gentleman musicians tell me that I must be very careful in supplying these two vacancies, which I have been two years in endeavouring to do." [1]

His efforts certainly met with the reward which they deserved, for we find the annual performance of music on St. Cecilia's Day growing more and more ambitious, until it reached a climax of excellence in 1731.

Of this service Mrs. Delaney, wife of Dr. Delaney

[1] Letter, February 9, 1719–20.

of the Cathedral Chapter, wrote to her sister that St.
Cecilia's Day was celebrated with great pomp in St.
Patrick's :—

> " We were there in the greatest crowd I ever saw ;
> we went in at ten and stayed till four.   There is a
> very fine organ. [As we noticed, it had been
> overhauled and enlarged the previous year.]
> [It] was accompanied by a great many instru-
> ments, Dubourg at the head of them : they began
> with the first concerto of Corelli ; we had Purcell's
> Te Deum and Jubilate ; then the fifth concerto
> of Corelli ; after that an anthem of Dr. Blow's,
> and they concluded with the eighth concerto of
> Corelli."

The preacher at this extensive performance was
Dr. Thomas Sheridan, a divine whose sermons seem
usually to have served more to his own disadvantage
than to the edifying of others.   On this occasion his
remarks about Presbyterians and Church music brought
down the wrath of the Dissenters upon his head, and
strong words were said about " the merrymaking
worship at the Cathedral on St. Cecilia's day ", and
about musical festivals " that turned a Christian
Church into a playhouse ".

It was this same Sheridan who had the bad luck to
choose the text " Sufficient unto the day is the evil
thereof " on the day of the accession of the Hanoverians,
and thereby to lose his chaplaincy.   Actually the
sermon was a well-worn non-political one out of his
stock in hand !   " Poor Sheridan ", said Swift, " by
mere chance medley, shot his own fortune dead with a
single text.".[1]   " What business ", said Swift to him,

---

[1] Swift, *Vindication of Lord Carteret*, Scott's Edition,
Vol. VII, p. 303.

L

quoting Don Quixote, " had you to speak of a halter
in a family where one of it was hanged ? " [1]

The salient points of that whole great St. Cecilia's
Day service were summed up neatly by Swift in half
a dozen lines :—

" Grave Dean of St. Patrick's, how comes it to pass,
That you who know music no more than an ass;
That you who so lately were writing of Drapiers,
Should lend your Cathedral to players and scrapers ?
To set such an opera once in a year,
So offensive to every true protestant ear."

If the truth were known, probably the inspiration
of the Cathedral choir derived entirely from the driving-
force of Swift's own enthusiasm. This was in spite
of little personal musical capacity. He derived no
great enjoyment from music, and he affected an entire
ignorance of the subject. In 1711 he wrote to Stella
from Windsor to tell how he had gone into the musical
meeting where he had often been desired to go, " but
was weary in half an hour of their fine stuff, and stole
out so privately, that everybody saw me ".

Naturally, as we might expect of him, he had no
patience with the occasional absurdities of musical
fashions. But if he had no ear, he had at least a
devastatingly clear and humorous common sense.
His friend Delaney relates with delight how once at
the Deanery he parodied the flamboyant style of
Thomas Roseingrave's playing with a vocal imitation
which much entertained his friends, but scandalized
poor Provost Pratt, " who was far gone in the Italian
taste ".[2] And he held the mirror up to his singing-
men and composers, and allowed them to see their
little affectations as others saw them, when he wrote

[1] Letter to Sheridan, September 11, 1725.
[2] Delaney, *Observations*, p. 149.

and insisted on performing his " Cantata "—a delightful
skit on contemporary music.

In the Cathedral choir, as in all departments of St.
Patrick's, Swift worked hard.   His rule was despotic—
but it obtained results.   Nothing less than perfection
would do Swift, and we shall see at the end of his career
the brilliance of that wonderful choir which sang to
Handel's accompaniment when " The Messiah " was
first performed in Dublin.

One of the finest traits of his character was the way
in which he could submerge his personal tastes and
inclination in favour of what would give beauty and
reverence to his great cathedral services.

This is nowhere clearer than in Swift's fine revealing
letter to Lady Carteret on the use of music in Divine
Service :—

> " For my own part, I would rather say my
> prayers without it.   But as long as it is thought
> by the skilful, to contribute to the dignity of public
> worship, by the blessing of God it shall never be
> disgraced by me; nor, I hope, by any of my
> successors."

CHAPTER X

SWIFT AND HANDEL

Handel and Dublin—His Music and St. Patrick's Choir—
Fashionable Dublin Musicians—Swift *versus* the Charitable
Musical Society—A Protest—Handel Comes to Ireland—
Rehearsals of the Messiah—First Performance—Swift's
Choristers—Swift and Handel Meet.

OF real, if pathetic interest, is the connection of Dean
Swift and his choir with Handel, the composer.

Handel had a strong Dublin connection; his oratorio,
"The Messiah", was written in order to be performed
by the Dublin Charitable Musical Society; he himself
conducted the first performance at Neal's Music Hall
in Fishamble Street; the old organ on which he played
is still shown at St. Michan's Church, Dublin, and he
visited Swift just before the Dean's death.

To-day Handel's "Messiah" is a favourite with
both the Cathedral choirs. It is often heard at Christmas and Easter and during Advent at St. Patrick's
and Christ Church.

In the eighteenth century Handel's fame came before
him to Dublin. The great composer did not arrive
in Dublin until the seventeen-forties, but his work
was popular for some years previously. For instance,
in April 1736 an anthem of Handel's was performed
in aid of Mercer's Hospital at the ancient Church of
St. Andrews by the Tholsel. The assistance of the
choirs of St. Patrick's and Christ Church was invoked
—mainly owing to a suggestion of Dean Swift and his

chapter, as a minute of the Governors of Mercer's hospital shows.

In a Dublin paper this performance was described—as a matter of fact, Handel appears to have been good copy, judging by the amount of publicity he obtained in contemporary news :—

> " On Thursday last was preached a charity sermon at St. Andrews by the Reverend Dean Madden, for the benefit of Mercer's Hospital; at the same time was performed a grand Te Deum Jubilate and an Anthem compos'd by the famous Mr. Handel. . . .
>
> " The principal voices were Mr. Church, Mr. Lamb, Mr. Bailys and Mr. Mason."

Three of these were gentlemen of St. Patrick's choir : Mr. Church we have already noticed when his behaviour was less creditable.

The report goes on to note that the peformers were over seventy in number, among whom were several " Noblemen and Gentlemen of Distinction ".

Skill in music was a fashionable attainment in eighteenth-century Dublin. Most of the élite of the city belonged to the Charitable Musical Society, a club which originally met in the Bull's Head Tavern in Fishamble Street, but moved to more imposing quarters when Neal's Music Hall was completed in 1714. At this society Lord Mornington performed on the violin and harpsichord, Lord Lucan played the flute and the Earl of Bellamont played the violoncello. Phenomenal sums of money were raised for charitable causes, and almost every week *Faulkiner's Journal* recorded the release of dozens and scores of debtors from prison by the bounty of the Society. (The immediate successor of this club, another Charitable

Musical Society of the same name, was founded in the seventeen-fifties, and it still flourishes. Its offices are in Schoolhouse Lane, behind Molesworth Street, Dublin.)

In 1741 two interesting things happened. First— Swift fell foul of the Society. Second—Handel was invited to Dublin.

What the explanation of the former may have been, no one will now know for certain. Probably the truth was that Swift, roused for a moment from the terrible throbbing lethargy which was paralysing his brain, heard that his beloved choir was performing in the Bull's Head Tavern, and jumped to the wrong conclusion. The result was that he wrote a bitter exhortation to his chapter calling on them to preserve the discipline of the choir. This document, dated January 28, 1741, was the last coherent thing that the unhappy old Dean ever wrote. Less than two months later guardians were appointed by the Court of Chancery to look after his affairs, and he was adjudged a lunatic.

Here is the exhortation—peevish, perhaps, but showing still a care for his choir that was both proud and personal :—

> " Whereas my infirmity and ill health have prevented me to preside in the Chapters held for the good order and government of my Cathedral Church of St. Patrick's, Dublin," it begins. [He had heard that various members of the Choir had assisted at public musical performances, and he would not allow it.] " And whereas it has been reported that I gave a licence to certain vicars to assist at a club of fiddlers in Fishamble Street, I hereby declare that I remember no such license to have ever been signed or sealed by me; and

that if ever such pretended license be produced,
I do hereby annul and vacate the said licence;
entreating my said Sub-Dean to punish such vicars
as shall ever appear there as songsters, fiddlers,
pipers, trumpeters, drummers, drum majors, or in
any sonal quality, according to the flagitious
aggravations of their respective disobedience,
rebellion, perfidity and in gratitude. I require
my said Sub-Dean to proceed to the extremity of
expulsion if the said vicars should be found un-
governable, impenitent or self-sufficient. . . . My
resolution is to preserve the dignity of my station
and the honour of my Chapter; and, gentlemen,
it is incumbent upon you to aid me, and to show
who and what the Dean and Chapter of St. Patrick's
are."

Meanwhile, the second event was taking place—
the Lord Lieutenant's invitation was being extended
to Handel—and, despite Swift's rebuke, the gentlemen
of Fishamble Street were planning to use his choir for
a remarkably brilliant performance in their new
headquarters which was now rapidly approaching
completion.

On November 18, 1741, Handel arrived in Dublin
with his recently completed score of " The Messiah ".
Three days afterwards the trustees of Mercer's Hospital
(among whom was Dr. Wynne, Sub-dean of St.
Patrick's) invited Handel to give an organ recital in
St. Andrew's Church.

Immediately plans went forward to produce " The
Messiah ". Both the Cathedral choirs were to take
part, and the best talent of Dublin was to assist.
Handel began preliminary rehearsals, and the singers
and instrumentalists were trained assiduously by the
irascible but efficient German. The final rehearsals

were awaited eagerly. The advertisement columns
of *Faulkiner's Journal* give considerable space to these,
one announcement quaintly providing us with information about the rival claims of music and a *cause célèbre*
on the interest of the general public :

> " The Rehearsal of Mr. Handell's sacred Oratorio
> called ' The Messiah ' will certainly be on Wednes-
> day the 1st day of February, at 12 o'clock at noon,
> at the Musick Hall in Fishamble Street, and if
> Lord Netterville's trial should come on the Friday
> following, the Performance will be postponed to a
> further Day. . . . Tickets to be had at half a
> guinea each."

The newspaper which appeared on the 4th of February
following noted that the rehearsal had been a great
success, but that owing to Lord Netterville's trial the
final one had been postponed until the 7th of the
month. A large crowd was expected, for ladies were
requested not to wear their hoops.

The first public performance was held on Tuesday,
April 13. Seven hundred people were present, and
more than £400 was collected in aid of " the Charitable
Infirmary, Mercer's Hospital and the Releasement of
Prisoners ".

" The Messiah " proved a wonderful success; it
was crowded at every performance with " a most Grand,
Polite and Crowded Audience ", or, as Handel noted,
with Nobility and Clergy : Bishops, Deans and " Heads
of the Colledge ". The newspapers—not so given to
superlatives as in modern times—went as far as to
exlaim that it was performed so well that it gave
" Universal Satisfaction " to all present, and that it
was allowed by the greatest Judges to be the finest
" Composition of Musick " that ever was heard !

Handel himself was charmed and the arduous days of rehearsals when he had quite lost his temper and gave way to Teutonic epithets were quite forgotten. Now he had nothing but praise for his performers, ranking high among whom were the massed choirs of Christ Church and St. Patrick's :—

> " The Basses and Counter Tenors are very good, and the rest of the Chorus Singers (by my Direction) do exceedingly well ".

Meanwhile Swift, in mental oblivion, tramped up and down the rambling staircases of the Deanery in a pathetic search for exercise which he imagined would restore his health.

But Swift's mind had gone for ever. When in August of 1742 Handel came to take his leave of the Dean, Swift had no idea who his caller was. At last his servant managed to make him remember something of Handel. " Oh, a German and a genius ! a prodigy ! " ejaculated Swift, memory returning in a weak spasm.[1]

So two great men met. We may imagine how Handel's compliments about the singing-men of St. Patrick's roused the helpless Dean for a moment from his stupor. Perhaps once again it gave him just a minute of glowing pride in that Choir for which he had laboured so diligently.[2]

[1] Mrs. Pilkington's Memoirs.
[2] On this chapter, see H. Townsend, *Handel in Dublin*, 1857.

CHAPTER XI

SWIFT THE PASTOR

THE time has come for us to follow the Dean out of the
stately dignity of the Cathedral into the hurly-burly
and the muddy, smoky streets of the Liberty of St.
Patrick's.

It is Sunday, and he is on his way home to the
Deanery from Morning Prayer. Perky little Mrs.
Pilkington shows him making the journey with considerable pomp. He marches sedately with the silver
verge carried before him.

> " And now, St. Patrick's saucy Dean
> With silver verge, and surplice clean ",

as one writer of doggerel describes it.

The journey was short, but, even so, it was expensive.
Before dinner the beggars must be tended, and a queue
of " regulars " waited for him outside the Cathedral.

For coming out of its broad doors, Swift passed into

his own little temporal kingdom. It was a compact, unsavoury realm—a close mass of small streets, comprising perhaps a hundred and fifty houses, " the Liberty of the Dean of St. Patrick's ".

(It must be explained that there were several " Liberties " in Dublin. These were semi-independent city districts, each with its own ruler and its own peculiar privileges.)

Here, in Patrick Street, New Street, Kevin Street, and Long Lane, as well as in the adjacent Liberties of the Archbishop and the Earl of Meath, lived the weavers of Dublin. Their looms worked in the big first-floor rooms of the Coombe, and in the houses all round the Cathedral. They were a community fairly industrious, thoroughly unbusinesslike, independent, and at times exuberantly riotous. Through their crowded alleys moved Swift, " absolute Monarch of the Liberties and King of the Mob ", as he said, idolized by these simple people, saluted by all, and conscientiously returning the bows of his parishioners until he wore out his hats before their time—he often said that the Liberties ought to pay him 40s. a year for wear and tear in beavers caused by acknowledging salutations !

Over the Cathedral Liberty Swift had titular jurisdiction. At one time the Deans of St. Patrick's had held their own law-courts. By Swift's time these had long ceased to exist, but nevertheless the Liberty remained more or less immune from outside interference.

This was unfortunate, because as a result St. Patrick's Liberty became a sanctuary for debtors, rogues and vagabonds, and a paradise for beggars. All sorts of penniless folk drifted there—not only Irish paupers, but unfortunates of all nationalities. Thus, among

Cathedral charities are donations to "Mr. Peter Delahay, a poor distress'd foreigner," and sundry gifts to a persistent pair of Hebrews, Abraham Jacob and Judah Abraham.[1]

The Dublin beggars were notoriously a lawless and undesirable body, resisting even Swift's efforts to badge them and to discipline them into some sort of order. The Dean continued to appoint his law officer, the Seneschal, though the duties of that official were slight and his authority must have been little. On occasion we read of the Cathedral itself having been robbed and the bells damaged, and Swift's beadle got into serious trouble for allowing some of the velvet cushions to disappear.[2]

Apart from this nomadic class of ne'er-do-wells, Swift's parishioners worked reasonably hard at their business, and they received every possible assistance from their Dean. We read their advertisements in Dublin papers. For interest's sake one of these is worth quoting :—

" JOHN ESCHEE

Living at the Sign of the Coat and Breeches in St. Patrick's Close, Dublin, sells all sorts of Cloths, Druggets, German Serges and Sogathees; as also all sorts of Cloaths ready made at reasonable prices. N.B. Any person that deals with the said Eschee, will save 20 per cent." [3]

But occasionally hard times came even to the more industrious members of Swift's congregation. The Dean and Chapter dealt generously with them in such calamities. Many entries are extant in the Cathedral receipt books like that of March 1720—" Ordered that

[1] Proctor's Accounts, 1726, 1717, 1719.
[2] Chapter Minutes.
[3] Dublin Gazette, January 7, 1728-9.

forty pounds be given to the poor weavers as their charity ", or a later one signed by Swift, " Payed the Dean, by order of the Dean and Chapter, five pounds, their charitable contribution towards relieving the many distressed poor families in St. Patrick's Liberties this severe frost ".[1]

Frost was not the only difficulty, nor the greatest one, with which Swift's weavers had to contend. Foreign competition, English policy, and sometimes their own incompetence caused frequent periods of trade depression. Many were the riots started in consequence by this independently minded community. One protest is described in *Pue's Occurrences* of May 31, 1735, when the figures of a man and a woman, dressed in " Calico and other Indian Goods ", were dragged in a cart to Market Square in the Coombe, and solemnly hanged from a Gibbet erected for the occasion. After this gesture the mob proceeded to St. Stephen's Green, where they draped the public gallows with similar stuff " to prevent these goods from being worn here ".

They were a full-blooded people, and they often seemed to fight for the mere love of fighting. Very serious indeed were the riots and party battles which occurred regularly. " The Ormond Boys and the Liberty Boys fought at St. James's Fair ", records a compressed news item of 1737. A modern Dublin paper would have been more generous of headlines, for these feuds between the weavers (the Liberty Boys) and the butchers and slaughterhouse-men (familiarly known as the Ormond Boys) were sensational and bloody affairs. In later years Charles Wesley was horror-struck by the brutality of these medleys,

[1] Proctor's Accounts, 1739.

when murder was often done, but all too rarely punished.

In the Dublin manufacturers' struggles against outside competition, Swift fought tooth and nail for the home industries. During the Economic War of his time the weavers of the Liberties fell into great distress. Their cloth became unsalable, and for a while the community fell to the starvation level. Funds were raised by wealthy Dubliners in order to help them, and a play was produced for their benefit, to which Swift contributed his share of jingling lines :—

> " We'll dress in manufactures made at home,
> Equip our Kings and gen'rals at the Comb.
> We'll rig in Meath Street Egypt's haughty queen,
> And Antony shall court her in ratteen.
> In blue shallon shall Hannibal be clad,
> And Scipio trail an Irish purple plad."

It is only fair to say that not a little of the misery of the weavers was their own fault, and Swift must often have fumed with justifiable indignation at the foolish knavishness and lack of business sense displayed by his adopted people.

The cry of the day was—as it is now—" Support Home Industries ! " Swift himself coined a phrase which survived in a disturbed Ireland as late as the twentieth century—" Burn everything English except their coal ". And all through Ireland the wearing of Irish-made clothes was pushed with lusty propaganda.

That was a policy which in itself was sound, and which might have been successful at the time, had the home industries been in any way efficient, or if they had even been willing to learn to give honest value. Unfortunately, the Irish workman of Swift's day did every job as if it were to be his last, preferring to charge exorbitantly, and to cheat if needs be, rather than to look forward to a repetition of custom. He did not care whether he ever got another order from the same customer; goodwill counted nothing to him. He preferred to seize the golden eggs at once, even if it meant killing the goose. And the textile industry failed badly in this respect. It was notoriously dishonest, nor would it pay any attention to Swift's suggestions for reform.

One proposal made by the Dean was this—that a group of manufacturers should join together to advertise their cloths and stuffs at fixed retail prices, and of guaranteed width and quality, " So that if a child of ten years old were sent with money, and directions what cloth or stuff to buy, he should not be wronged in any one article ".[1] This scale of fixed prices should be accompanied by a money-back guarantee, signed by all members of the association of manufacturers. If any one member should default in any respect, he would render himself liable to immediate public expulsion from the group.

Nothing could be better calculated to restore the credit of the Irish manufacturers in the eyes of the public. Very naturally (as Swift pointed out) when gentlemen and ladies were cheated once or twice in the sale of Irish cloth, they did what both in prudence and resentment they ought to do, and bought imported English goods. Swift's suggestion was the obvious one under the circumstances.

But, alas ! for Swift and his well-meant plans, the local tradesmen of St. Patrick's Close and the Coombe would not reform. They could not be induced to abandon their pathetic belief in quick profits, and let

[1] Swift, *Observations on The Case of the Woollen Manufacturers.*

the purchaser beware. To improve trade conditions, they preferred to rely on the time-honoured methods of raising riots, burning effigies, and writing scurrilous letters to the papers !

Swift's practical mind prepared another plan. A deputation of weavers had again waited on him, demanding, as usual, that someone should do something for the woollen trade, and why should the Archbishop not make his clergy wear Dublin-made gowns ?

" Certainly ", replied Swift, " I shall speak to the Archbishop. And what is more, I shall arrange to collect with him at the Palace as many clergy as I can bring together, in order that they may see your samples for themselves. Kindly prepare some black woollen material to sell at about eightpence a yard, and if it is satisfactory, I have no doubt that the Archbishop will press the matter with his clergy at the coming Visitation."

The manufacturers retired, apparently highly delighted on the surface, but probably murmuring within themselves that the good Dean knew nothing about business. For when the time came, nothing happened. They did not return until a fortnight after the appointed day, and when they did come it was with a different plan, which seemed to them both original and effective—namely, that Swift should write a rousing pamphlet in support of the wearing of home manufactures ! The Dean inquired about his samples of eightpenny black stuff. The manufacturers smiled— they knew better than to waste their time with samples ! None had been prepared, nor were ever likely to be.[1]

It was against ignorance and obstinacy of this sort

[1] Swift, *A Letter to the Archbishop of Dublin Concerning the Weavers.*

that the keen mind of Swift had to contend in his fight for the betterment of the people whom he loved— for Swift loved his flock, even though he could not help being angry at their stupidity and bestiality. They idolized him, this Drapier whose pen had defeated the power of England. He in his turn fought for them, his brain at white heat with indignation against the systems which had so degraded them. He burned to see his simple people treated with justice, yet he could not help loathing their sordid fecklessness with anger and disgust.

He loved and he hated at the same time. So we find that strange picture of the devoted pastor who laboured indefatigably doing kindnesses with a stern, set face, generous beyond all expectation, bitterly hard on animal filth and sloth.

With a queer instinct, his people understood him, and, while fearing him, they adored him too. He could handle these difficult, indecisive folk, and they knew it. They respected him and they loved him for it. It was a hard, autocratic method which Swift adopted, but with his low-class people perhaps it was the only possible one. That may well be part of the reason for the ugly violence of his language in a letter to a parishioner about her undutiful daughter, still preserved in Trinity College, Dublin.[1] (Undoubtedly Swift's mad fastidiousness was another part of the reason, too.) Very unlovely the wording was, but it was probably effective. These people were people who answered only to the language of a master, and they had to be made to obey.

At any rate, they seem to have loved him none the less for it. When he came back from the country he

[1] Letter to Mrs. Swanton, Peter St., July 12, 1733.

M

was escorted home to the Deanery with cheers and great rejoicing. His seventieth-birthday celebrations were kept with delirious gladness.

" There were Bonfires, Illuminations, Firing of Guns, etc. Many loyal Healths were drank; Long Life to the Drapier; Prosperity to poor Ireland; and to the Liberty of the Press." [1]

We can see the crowds intoxicated with delight dancing round the leaping red flames of blazing tar-barrels, shouting for their Dean. And behind the Deanery curtains we can see a brightening of the old man's dull eyes.

They would do anything for him, believe anything he chose to say. There is a typical story of a crowd which had assembled to view an eclipse. Swift sent out a bellman to announce that the eclipse had been postponed by the Dean's orders. Whereupon the crowd promptly dispersed.

How did he gain this popularity? Partly by his successful defence of the Irish people in the Drapier letters. But that was not the whole secret. He won their respect and their liking, and finally their love, by his wonderful pastoral work and by his charity.

Swift combined a rather exaggerated meanness with a wonderful generosity. Indeed, the reason why he was sparing in his own needs was in order that he might give more adequately to those in want.

It is said that he gave away one-third of his income to charity and that he would part with £5 more easily than another would with 5s. Certainly he gave very freely to necessitous friends and poor relations. The *Journal* is full of notes of quite unself-conscious gifts

[1] *Pue's Occurrences*, December 4, 1736.

May the 15th 1736

I promise to pay to our Martha
Whiteway for the use of her Son
John Whiteway, whenever he
becomes to some able Chirurgian
a Prentice, and Six Months after
he is bound apprentice to the sd
Chirurgian, the Sum of one
hundred pounds Sterl, as a
Reward or fine, to be given to
the sd Chirurgian for receiving
the sd John Whiteway for his
Apprentice, and for teaching him
the Art of Chirurgery Witness
my hand and Seal this fifteenth
day of May 1736 — Six

Witnesses present. Jonath: Swift
signed and Seald in the presence of
Roger Kendrick
Alexr Broadery

SWIFT'S HANDWRITING.

[Facing p. 169

given to down-and-out acquaintances, like that " poor poet, one Mr. Diaper, in a nasty garret, very sick," whom he noted in the *Journal* to Stella.   He gave Mrs. Dingley an annuity of £52 a year, gravely surrounding the gift with legal fictions in order to persuade her that it came from an investment of her own.   Throughout her lifetime he financed his sister Jane, who had married badly.   Examples of this kind of generosity are frequent.   Deserving (and often undeserving) authors gained considerable help from the Dean. Mrs. Pilkington and Mrs. Barber owed a great deal to his kindness.   The former tells of the gift of a slice of plum cake, stuffed with five golden plums—Swift's way of giving five guineas.   He compiled the auto-biography of the broken-down Captain Creighton in order to help him with a few pounds from the publishers. As a matter of fact, Swift seems to have given away the profits of all his publications except *Gulliver*.   Both to strangers and to friends he was more than generous. The writer recently discovered an autograph letter by Swift, guaranteeing £100 to Mrs. Whiteway for the apprenticing of her son.   As this has not previously been published, it may be worth quoting :—

" May the 15th, 1736.   I promise to pay to Mrs. Martha Whiteway for the use of her son John Whiteway, whenever he becomes to some able Chirurgian a Prentice, and Six Months after he is bound apprentice to the sd. Chirurgian, the sum of one hundred pounds sterl. as a Reward or fine to be given to the sd. Chirurgian for recieving the sd. John Whiteway for his Apprentice, and for teaching him the Art of Chirurgery.   Witness my hand and seal this fifteenth day of may 1736— six. . . . Jonath. Swift."

A facsimile illustration of this document is given. The gift was confirmed by his will, with an additional £5 for medical books.

Charity was not confined to his own friends and relations; he had also a wonderfully organized personal scheme of parish relief, mostly at his own expense.

His friend Delaney gives a vivid picture of the Dean's charity. He was the perfect " walking parson ", constantly striding round the streets of Dublin in order that he might see the conditions of the poor and relieve them when necessary. " Here ", said Delaney, " he literally followed the example of his blessed Saviour and went about doing good ".[1]

Mrs. Brent, his housekeeper, described Swift's method of being charitable—" which is, to debar himself of what he calls the superfluities of life, in order to administer to the necessities of the distressed ". Thus, when he saved a coach-fare by making the journey on foot, the money preserved went to some poor cripple. On the same system, he drank beer for dinner instead of wine—and then gave away the price of a pint of wine to some destitute old woman.

Mrs. Pilkington gives a spirited picture of the scheme in action. She and Swift had arrived back at the Deanery just in time to escape a shower, and consequently they avoided taking a coach.

" Thank God ! " said the Dean, " I have saved my money; here you fellow " (to his servant) " carry this sixpence to the lame old man that sells gingerbread at the corner, because he tries to do something and does not beg." [2]

In order to provide suitably for each case, Swift

[1] Delaney's *Observations*.
[2] Mrs. Pilkington's *Memoirs*.

collected coins of all values—as he wandered round the city he carried a pocket full of everything from a threepenny piece to a crown,[1] and the money was dispensed freely. Not that Swift allowed himself to be imposed upon—he was discriminating in his charity and only gave when he felt it was deserved. Mrs. Pilkington describes that typical Sunday morning after service, when he gave to a whole crowd of beggars— except for one old woman whose hand when held out proved to be very dirty indeed. Swift remarked pungently that although she was a beggar, " water was not so scarce but that she might have washed her hands ". Doubtless by the next Sunday she had learnt the virtue of cleanliness.

The condition of the poor at that time was extraordinarily bad; Berkeley went as far as to query in 1736, " Whether there be upon Earth any Christian or Civilized People so beggarly wretched and destitute as the common Irish? "[2] Swift's efforts for the Dublin poor must have been a godsend, especially for the honest, industrious sort. (Even he could do little for some of the worst of the professional riff-raff, who looked on it as a deadly insult to be decked with a badge and a number.) His charities were recognized by his acquaintances as being " wise and extensive ",[3] and they gave splendid assistance to the decent poor folk who really did need assistance.

He was particularly interested in the progress of the young and the advancement of struggling tradesmen. Many were the lads educated and apprenticed by Swift's aid. In 1716 he had started a charity school for boys,

[1] Delaney, *Observations*, p. 9.
[2] Berkeley, *The Querist*, p. 132.
[3] Mrs. Delaney's *Journals*, 1861 Ed., Vol. I, p. 64.

children of the poorer inhabitants of the Cathedral
precincts, and during the same year he preached a
charity sermon for their benefit.[1]   Many of these boys,
when they had completed their education, were apprenticed to shopkeepers at Swift's expense, like the two
sons of " Mary Curvillio, widow in great distress and
want," who received £2 10s. apiece to bind them
" apprentice to Protestant Masters ".[1]

One of the crushing difficulties of many poor tradesmen was the impossibility of raising the small lump
sum necessary to buy tools and stock in trade.   Swift
saw that there was a very real need here, and since his
object was, as Delaney inscribed on a piece of plate,

> " Not strolling idleness to aid,
> But honest industry decayed ",

he resolved to make it possible for this class to raise
themselves in the world.

His idea was to form a sort of private bank, giving
out on loan small sums of money, to be repaid free of
interest over a period of twelve months, at the rate of
2s. for each £5.   This he did with the first unencum-
bered £500 which he ever possessed.

Probably there were occasional failures.   No doubt
one or two of the beggarly crew of the Liberty said to
themselves that " such a Fine Gentleman as the Dean
would not be wanting money back from a poor man,
and sure Doctor Swift has so much that he won't miss
it ", and so defaulted in the repayments.   Then, when
Swift had to take the drastic steps of calling upon the
guarantor to pay the money back, of course he was the
meanest usurer that ever lived !   Nobody then considered that if the money were not repaid regularly, the

[1] Chapter Minutes, 1716.

scheme could not carry on at all. Dealings with the low-class Irish were not uncommonly heartbreaking. But on the whole the scheme worked well. It continued for years to put small tradesmen on their feet, despite Dr. Johnson's statement that it had to be dropped almost as soon as begun.[1]

As housekeeper in the Deanery, Mrs. Brent was in a position to give the verdict of a sensible woman. And what she says sounds conclusive.

" You cannot imagine what numbers of poor tradesmen who have even wanted proper tools to carry on their work, have, by this small loan, been put in a prosperous way and brought up their families in credit."

Now we must allow Doctor Delaney to speak further for himself about Swift's pastoral care of his flock :—

" I never saw poor so carefully and conscientiously attended to in my life, as those of his Cathedral; they were lodged, and never begged out of their district; and they always appeared with a very distinguished decency and cleanliness; and after some time partly by collecting charities, but more by contributing, he got a little alms house built and furnished, with a few of the most ancient and orderly widows, in one of the closes of his cathedral, where they lived with a decency and cleanliness equal to that of the best English Poor, which he took care to keep up, by frequent visits to them in person." [2]

In the nearby streets dwelt Swift's " seraglio "—the poor old women who could not have lived but for the ready shillings which came from Swift's deep waistcoat

[1] Johnson, *Lives of the English Poets, Swift.* C. F. Mason, *St. Patrick's,* p. 417, for opposite.
[2] Delaney, *Observations,* p. 6.

pocket. Here lived " Stumpa-Nympha ", without
arms or legs; Flora, who sold bunches of violets;
Cancerina; Stumpantha; Pullagowna, who plucked
at his coat-tails and begged for sixpence. The Dean
had a warm corner in his heart for these poor old pieces
of human debris, and many a time they must have
climbed painfully up the Deanery steps and tugged at
the bell. Woe betide any footman who ignored one of
these old ladies ! At least one hard-hearted servant
was discharged at a moment's notice by a furious
Dean because he had refused to convey the petition of
an old woman who had waited on the steps for him
one bitter frosty morning.

How Swift delighted in their pathetic little handi-
crafts ! At least they were trying to earn an honest
living, and that counted for so much with him.

" He kept strictly to that Turkish principle of
honouring none, but such as were bred up, and
occupied in some laudable employment. One of
these mistresses sold plumbs; another, hob nails;
a third, tapes; a fourth, ginger-bread; a fifth,
knitted; a sixth, darned stockings; and a seventh,
cobbled shoes; and so on beyond my counting.

" One of these mistresses wanted an eye;
another, a nose; a third, an arm; a fourth, a foot.

" He saluted them with all becoming kindness;
asked them how they did, how they throve; what
stock they had etc.?

" If any of their wares were such, as he could
possibly make use of, or pretend to make use of,
he always bought same; and paid for every half-
pennyworth, at least sixpence; and for every
pennyworth, a shilling."

So writes Delaney.[1]

Swift wrote as a misanthrope, and he did detest with

[1] Delaney, *Observations*, p. 90.

unspeakable bitterness injustice, dishonesty and greed, sloth, dirt and idleness.

But he loved these simple souls very dearly indeed, and they loved him in their turn.

For Dean Swift was a very wonderful pastor.

.   .   .   .   .

After thirty-two years of deanship Swift laid aside his pastoral work for ever.

On Saturday, October 19, 1745, Swift passed away peacefully in the seventy-eighth year of his age. For two days his frail body lay in state in the Deanery hall, the dead face now gentle and placid, framed in a frosting of white, silky hair. And all day long his own people filed past his coffin, recalling the days of long ago when their Dean had walked among them.

As they passed by, one old friend bent down and cut a wisp of white hair from the quiet head, to preserve it for ever as a keepsake.

Only a very few friends were present three days later, when at midnight the tired body was laid to rest in the south side of the Nave of St. Patrick's.

He lies there still, keeping watch over his great Cathedral Church. Near his grave is a great slab of black marble, bearing the epitaph which he wrote for himself :—

" Hic depositum est corpus
JONATHAN SWIFT, S.T.D.
Hujus Ecclesia Cathedralis
Decani,
Ubi saeva Indignatio
Ulterius
Cor lacerare nequit.
Abi Viator
Et imitare, si poteris,
Strenuum pro virili
Libertatis Vindicatorem.
Obiit 19° die mensis Octobris,
A.D. 1745, Anno Aetatis 78°.

NOTE ON SOURCES

THE number of books about Swift is overwhelming, and the author's excuse for adding another to their number must be that anything about Swift's religion is extraordinarily rare. In the bibliography of a recent life—Ricardo Quintana's *The Mind and Art of Jonathan Swift* (1936)—out of more than two hundred works about Swift recorded, only two dealt with his religion. When we consider that Swift was Dean of a great Cathedral for thirty-two years, the omission is surprising. This book attempts to supplement other works, in order to give a balanced estimate of Swift's character.

Three modern works, one large, two small, deal directly with the subject. The first is *La Pensée Religieuse de Swift et ses Antinomies*, by M. le Chanoine C. Looten, published in 1935. This book does less than justice to Swift, since the author fails to fit him into his proper place in conjunction with eighteenth-century religious and political ideas. It also fails to probe beneath the oddities which masked Swift's real religious feelings from the world.

Two other short articles by clergy of the Church of Ireland are altogether admirable. One is " Dean Swift as a Churchman " by the Reverend G. F. Hamilton (*Irish Church Quarterly*, July 1917). To this paper the present author is deeply indebted for hints at the beginning of his work. The other study of Swift's religion, " The Religion of Dean Swift ", was published in the *English Church Quarterly* for July 1938, and is

from the pen of Professor Jourdan.   It appeared just
as the present book was completed.

There are standard biographies in abundance.
Recently there has been one almost every year—some
friendly, some hostile; some excellent, others not so
good.   Shane Leslie, Stephen Gwynn, Rossi and Hone,
Van Doren, Ricardo Quintana and Bernard Newman
are among the biographers of the last decade.   The
first three of these writers, however, miss the real
Swift in their interpretations, which seem to the author
of this book quite unsatisfactory.   All of them would
make Swift a hypocrite—and hypocrisy is a trait which
was absolutely foreign to the man.   Probably the best
of these six books are Quintana's *Mind and Art of
Jonathan Swift* (1936) and Newman's *Jonathan Swift*
(1937).   The latter gives a very good summary of
Swift's religion.   Lord Longford's play, *Yahoo*, also
deserves mention as a thoroughly scholarly study.

In point of fact, the present writer has taken most
of his material from Swift's own works and letters,
from early biographies, and from sources in St. Patrick's
Cathedral archives.   The splendidly annotated edition
of Swift's Correspondence by J. Elrington Ball proved a
real mine of information, as did Archbishop Bernard's
Introduction.   For the other works of Swift, Sir Walter
Scott's 1824 Edition has principally been used.

About half a score of early biographers between them
provide the majority of the available facts.   The first
was the Earl of Orrery, whose *Remarks* of 1752, somewhat spiteful in tone, are chiefly valuable because they
called forth such a splendid reply in Delaney's *Observations on Lord Orrery's Remarks* (1754).   Dr. Patrick
Delaney was rector of St. Werburgh's Church, near
Hoey's Court, a friend and contemporary of Swift,

and a member of his Cathedral Chapter. Probably he is our best authority. Other illuminating information from the period is that given by Mrs. Pilkington. Her *Memoirs* (1748) are very highly coloured, but there seems no reason to doubt their substantial accuracy.

The next book in period of time, Deane Swift's *Essay upon the Life, Writings and Character of Dr. Jonathan Swift* (1756), was recognized by contemporaries to be a fantastic unreliable work.

Coming a little later, Sheridan's *Life of Swift* (1785) is reasonably sound, but very dull.

The fullest information of all is given in that massive monument to industry by W. Monck Mason, *The History and Antiquities of the Collegiate and Cathedral Church of St. Patrick* (1820). It is a storehouse of information. Its two great defects are the lack of an index and an exaggerated partisanship in favour of Swift. For all that, it is still perhaps the fullest source for almost everything about Swift.

Sir William Wilde's little book, *The Closing Years of Dean Swift's Life* (1849) is useful; it is still recognized by modern medical authorities as giving substantially accurate information about Swift's ailments.

For his early years Forster's *Life of Swift* (1875) has been consulted. Two other books always on the author's desk have been Sir Henry Craik's *Life*, and Sir Leslie Stephen's *Swift*, both published in 1882.

W. E. H. Lecky's essay, " Swift," in *Leaders of Public Opinion in Ireland* (1861) has been most suggestive on the subject of the relationship of Swift's politics and his religion.

Two early books which have been stimulating in their hostility are Dr. Johnson's *Lives of the English Poets*, and Thackeray's study in *The English Humorists* (1850).

Much of the material has been gathered in and around the walls of St. Patrick's Cathedral, Dublin. Archbishop Bernard's little book on the Cathedral (Bell's Cathedral Series) is an excellent guide. The writer must also thank the Dean of St. Patrick's for access to the manuscript archives of the Cathedral, particularly to contemporary Receipt Books and Chapter Minutes. He also records his indebtedness for the use of the delightful Deanery scrapbooks.

Eighteenth-century Dublin newspapers have proved fruitful sources of information and of local colour about the period. For the background of old Dublin, and for many hints about Swift's surroundings and contemporaries, Constantia Maxwell's *Dublin Under the Georges* is excellent. For Irish Church history, Mant, Olden, and Allison Phillips have been useful; J. R. Greene and G. R. Balleine (*History of the Evangelical Party*) have also helped.

Lastly, the author must thank the Reverend Rowland Athey, Rector of Trim, for information about Laracor, Miss Fitzgerald of the Church Body Library for copies of Meath Diocesan documents, William Mitchell, Esq., of Castlefleming, Leix, for permission to reproduce an autograph letter by Swift which he recently found in his home, Archdeacon Healy and Philip O'Connell, Esq., for living traditions about Swift, and T. H. Mason, Esq., and the National Gallery of Ireland for permission to reproduce illustrations.

APPENDIX

To the technical psychologist the whole subject of Swift's mental composition is a matter of extreme interest. In the text of this book nothing more has been attempted than to indicate some of the contradictory ingredients which united in the making of a very complex personality. However, Canon G. W. Murray (of Clonmel, Co. Tipperary), who is an expert psychologist, has kindly given the writer some very interesting notes which add much to the subject from the scientific point of view. The following is a brief abstract of his findings.

It is almost certain, he says, that the circumstances surrounding Swift's infancy are responsible for much that seems strange in his after-life. He belongs to a clearly defined type which seeks the satisfaction of an emotion grounded on a mother complex. This is a type which avoids the crucial problem of marriage, and which results from thwarted mother-love in infancy. It is especially aggravated when the infant affections are constantly transferred to nurses or mother-substitutes. (As we have seen, this does seem to have been the case in Swift's own infancy, when for three years he lived with the family nurse at Whitehaven.)

As a rule, other complications are present, and the case of Swift is no exception. He was a man driven by mental processes over which at times he could keep no control whatsoever—herein lay his tragedy. Thus,

every infant passes through a phase in which a
peculiar interest is taken in certain natural processes.
It is unfortunately possible for an unsympathetic
parent or nurse to deal with this normal and transitory
stage of development in so drastic a manner as to
create a fixation which may very seriously affect
subsequent life. In accordance with individual re-
actions and the manner in which they were brought
about, the resulting adult may become careless as
regards dress and personal cleanliness, or on the other
hand he may exhibit a passion for washing and an
abnormal repugnance for dust and dirt. Physical re-
actions are frequently set up, a very common example
being the vertigo from which Swift suffered. But
these are trivial matters compared with the check
which may be given to sex-development. In extreme
cases inhibition against marriage will result. The
evidence that Swift suffered from such a fixation is
overwhelming. His marriage with Stella was brought
about only by the complications of a double entangle-
ment. He had found himself loved by two women—a
position which perhaps he had not so much sought, as
failed to avoid. The growing and unwelcome passion
of Vanessa was quite outside Swift's control, and his
correspondence with her shows how he did his best to
curb it. Eventually he was forced into a marriage of
desperation, the result of which would be in complete
accord with the remark of the Archbishop of Dublin
to Dr. Delaney (as reported by Scott), " You have just
met the most unhappy man on earth, but on the
subject of his wretchedness you must never ask a
question ".

On this hypothesis it is easy to reconcile Swift's
fastidiousness in conversation and personal cleanliness

with the coarseness which is found in his writings. Each belongs to a different category. For him the obscene was doubly hurtful, and the horror of dirt wounded him where the normal man would have ignored it. As regards marriage, though he was fully developed physically, mentally he was inhibited. In this he may be likened to a hungry man who has been forced to sit down to a cannibal feast. A child reared among cannibals would have no qualms in helping himself from the common pot, and he would be at a loss to understand why anyone should object. (Swift's little suggestion for using up superfluous children might be taken as an example of quite a logical argument on the subject !) The inhibition of civilized man is purely mental, but that does not make it any the less final. Most people reared in these countries would prefer starvation to cannibalism, and in Swift's case the inhibition against marriage was in every way as strong.

INDEX